MYTH, RACE AND POWER

South Africans Imaged on Film and TV

Critical Studies in African Anthropology
Number 1

MYTH, RACE AND POWER

South Africans Imaged on Film and TV

by

KEYAN TOMASELLI

ALAN WILLIAMS

LYNETTE STEENVELD

RUTH TOMASELLI

Anthropos Publishers
Bellville
1986

Copyright c 1986 by
Keyan Tomaselli, Alan Williams,
Lynette Steenveld and Ruth Tomaselli

ANTHROPOS PUBLISHERS
P.O. Box 636
7530 Bellville
SOUTH AFRICA

ISBN 0 620 09003 0

Typed by Folio Typing Bureau, Bellville
Printed by Mills Litho (Pty) Ltd, Cape Town

Critical Studies in African Anthropology

General Editor

Frans H. Boot, University of the Western Cape

CONTENTS

FOREWORD

ABOUT THE SERIES

The aim of the series is to promote critical analysis of the African, and particularly the Southern African scene. The extent of this scene is viewed comprehensively and includes government, industry, education, sport, religion, art, communication (film, radio, press), 'development' and whatever activity and institution in which the interplay between race, language, culture, class and ethnic group is reflected. It is argued that the impasse in which the Continent finds itself cries out for fresh and critical thought and action. The editor and the contributing authors to this series feel that for too long scientific and academic endeavour have been artifically separated from reality. Instead of the classical subject-object dichotomy, the aim of the approach here proposed would bring a committed, concerned and human approach to the analysis of the problems of the African continent. To pursue this aim the editor wishes to promote the questioning and analysis of the epistemological background of policies, paradigms, doctrines and ideologies, and their relation to the 'reality on the ground'. Each analyst will of necessity depart from a particular point of view - by so doing he/she in turn becomes part of the on-going process of critical and evaluative analysis and action.

ABOUT THE AUTHORS

Keyan Tomaselli is Professor and Director of the Contemporary Cultural Studies Unit, University of Natal, Durban. He has taught film and television production, theory and criticism in the Department of Journalism and Media Studies, Rhodes University, and before that in the School of Dramatic Art, University of the Witwatersrand. Professor Tomaselli has made over 154 films and videos and has been the invited guest at three international film festivals. He is the author of numerous internationally published articles on film. He has published two books, including **Race and Class in South African Cinema** to be published in Chicago early in 1986.

Alan Williams is an Honours graduate of the Department of Journalism and Media Studies of Rhodes University. One of his undergraduate majors was Social Anthropology. Mr Williams specialised in film and television and is presently working as a video producer.

Lynette Steenveld studied in London. She began her career as a school teacher and then obtained a Post Graduate Diploma in Journalism and Media Studies from Rhodes University. She is now lecturing in the Department and is assisting in the film and television courses.

Ruth Tomaselli is a Wits University Development Studies (MA) graduate. She is a freelance researcher and writer. She has written extensively on 'Indian' South African hawkers, media and culture. She is an Associate Editor of **Critical Arts: A Journal for Media Studies,** an editorial board member of **Transkei Development Review** and co-authors a media column in **Die Suid-Afrikaan.**

ABOUT THE BOOK

Myth, Race and Power : South Africans Imaged on Film and TV examines films and television series made by both local and overseas producers. Amongst the titles discussed in detail are Laurens van der Post's **Testament of the Bushmen,** various films made by John Marshall on the !Kung, the SABC's **They Came from the East** and the British made **White Tribe of Africa.**

The book is one of the few to deal with the subject of ethnographic and documentary film. Not only does it examine the existing tenets of this new area of study, but the authors have drawn on their extensive film production experience to develop a set of principles of ethnographic film production.

The authors discuss the very thin line between propaganda and documentary, and show how ethnographic films become propaganda in particular viewing contexts.

The book offers the most exhaustive bibliography and filmography available on South African ethnographic film.

ACKNOWLEDGEMENTS

We would like to thank the following for making this research possible: National Film Archives, SABC-TV, Department of Foreign Affairs and Information, Cape Provincial Film Library, Paul Bellinger and Astra Films for allowing us access to their film holdings, and in some cases, viewing facilities as well. The SABC and the Cape Provincial Library kindly provided us with viewer statistics.

We are indebted to Bill Nichols for his critical comments on many of the ideas contained in this study, and to Lionel Friedberg for granting us an interview. Thanks too, to Dr H C Marais and the HSRC referees for their critique of an earlier draft of this study.

The authors and publishers are grateful for permission to reproduce photographs from the following sources:

Department of Foreign Affairs and Information for photographs related to: 'To Act a Lie', 'White Roots in Africa', 'Rock Art Treasures', 'A Place Called Soweto'.

Rob Purdey for photographs from 'Future Roots'.

Paul Bellinger for photographs from 'A Testament to the Bushmen'.

Documentary Educational Resources and **John Marshall** for photographs from 'Nai: The Story of a !Kung Woman', 'The Hunters', and 'A Curing Ceremony'.

Financial assistance rendered by the Human Sciences Research Council through its Main Committee for the HSRC Investigation into Intergroup Relations for undertaking the research is hereby acknowledged. The views expressed in this work or the conclusions drawn are those of the writers and should not be regarded as those of the Human Sciences Research Council or the Main Committee of the HSRC into Intergroup Relations.

A NOTE ON STYLE

Following the practice adopted by many Anglo-Saxon social scientists, considerable use has been made of single quotation marks to emphasise certain words and phrases. The American convention is to continue to employ double quotation marks. The use of single quotation marks is, we believe, more efficient as it clearly marks the distinction between quotations and the use of words and phrases in a more general sense. Briefly, this device fulfills three basic functions: first, it may indicate to the reader that such words are not being used in their literal sense, but have metaphorical overtones. More often, however, it is used to distance the authors from words which do not form part of their ideological vocabulary, but are borrowed from other writers and commentators, and the social lexicon they imply. Used in this way, these words echo their sources and imply a rich background of imagery and connotation. Finally, the accentuating of words and phrases is a shorthand way of highlighting attitudes and ideologies, and holding them up to critical scrutiny.

This study has made extensive use of semiotic categories. Space prevents each of these concepts from being defined in the text. Where readers are in doubt they are referred to Eco (1976), Mercer (1979) and Fiske (1982) whose interpretations form the basis of this study.

PREFACE

The present volume is a lengthier version of a study originally conducted for the Human Sciences Research Council (HSRC) under the auspices of their Intergroup Relations Project. The study was done during the latter half of 1983 and the first half of 1984. It is also the outgrowth of many years of production experience and theoretical analysis on the part of the senior author who was the project leader for the HSRC study.

Very few books on the subject of ethnographic film have been written. Journal articles are few and far between, but the interest in this area of film-making has been growing annually since the early 1970s in America and Europe, and since 1980 in South Africa. This book scans existing ethnographic film theories and develops a rigorous theoretical framework which meshes the postulates of written anthropology with film theory. This framework is used to analyse existing films and to develop production principles to guide future ethnographic film-making.

Film books generally have a wide readership. This one is no different, though it will be of particular interest to anthropologists, ethnographers, sociologists, African studies, film and television students and producers and students of communication.

Chapter One examines the concept of myth, which is basic to an understanding of the analysis that follows. The second chapter offers an overview of ethnographic film theory, its genesis, problems and the different theoretical perspectives which co-exist and which are sometimes mutually exclusive. The theoretical discussion is grounded in empirical examples of films about South Africans. This pattern is maintained throughout the book. We have tried to explicate our theory through examples in the later chapters, making the task of the reader easier.

The book has an extensive index, bibliography and filmography. This alone should make it useful as a resource that will aid research in a variety of disciplines. It should be of interest to non-academics, such as archivists, film-makers, distributors and film libraries.

CHAPTER 1

ETHNOGRAPHIC FILM, MYTH AND SOCIETY

The study of film in the West has largely centred on Hollywood, on feature films, directors, producers, all within a narrative based film theory and criticism. The study of documentary has, until recently, been pushed aside and considered unimportant.

As early as the 1940s, John Grierson argued that documentary could lubricate the democratic process, making it a very powerful mass means of visual information. What did occur, particularly in South Africa - from the very beginning of documentary film production in the late 1890s - was distortion. Distortion of people, social relationships, culture, integrity and of individuals by film-makers. This occurred partly because film-makers were unaware of the power of their medium for misrepresentation. They were unaware of the inappropriate theories of society which informed their cinematic perspectives, and they were unaware of their ideological assumptions which shaped their production practices. Finally, the photograph assumed the mantle of the God's-eye-view: it was thought to show truth in all its visible clarity.

The film-maker assumed the mantle of God, and through the magic image, technologically and culturally dominant societies and classes imposed their interpretations on subject cultures being filmed by their representatives. In South Africa, most of the films about people made since the turn of the century, are a searing indictment of the commercial and ideological intentions and integrity of their film-makers. Geography, history, sociology and anthropology have all been distorted in the interests of political expediency.

South Africa's social and cultural milieu - like just about every sphere of her physical existence - is richly endowed with a dramatic diversity. This raw material, like gold, should have placed us at the forefront of ethnographic film production and theory. Yet film-makers and social scientists failed dismally in their task. The

National Film Archives will only keep the serious researcher busy for a couple of days. To discover most films on South Africans, one has to look to the archives of foreign television companies.

With the very late establishment of film and television courses - only in the late 1970s - little headway was made with regard to ethnographic film theory, and the application of this theory through production. The spearhead for this innovation was Dr John van Zyl of the School of Dramatic Art of the University of the Witwatersrand who, with the help of film-maker Keyan Tomaselli, infused ethnographic theory concepts into their film, video and photographic coursework. This was followed by an ethnographic film festival organised by the School in 1980 to which anthropologist/film-maker Jay Ruby of Temple University was invited.

Most films on South Africa have been made by the Department of Information. Depending on the political currents of the time the ideological discourse changed from 'blacks as savages', 'the Noble Savage civilised', 'blacks as human but different', to finally, blacks, paradoxically, as 'the same but different'. Outside of this continuum are the very recent films in which white film-makers communicate their social guilt as members of the dominant group responsible for the demise of 'the Bushmen'. This sense of guilt does not extend to films on other tribes or groups who have suffered from colonial and neo-colonial white exploitation.

This brief introduction will not provide an overview of South African history. It aims rather to articulate some of the basic intentions of the study that follows. We have tried through critical analysis of both films and existing ethnographic film theory to:

a)   examine the production practices and assumptions of specific film-makers;

b)   offer theoretically informed criticisms of films made on South Africans by both local and foreign film-makers. Our concern is primarily with the representation of 'black'-'white' relationships, and within that both South African and British images of Afrikaners, and 'white' South African perspectives of the descendants of Indian immigrants, and the 'Bushmen';

c) develop a theory of ethnographic film production. This attempt develops existing principles, but injects the discussion with a far more rigorous semiotic and historical materialist framework. It meshes **criticism** of existing films with actual **production** experience. The study, therefore,

d) begins to address the problem of paradigm incompatability between 'written anthropology' and that of 'a filmic ethnography'. In other words, this study examines South African films about people from the joint perspectives of anthropological and film theory.

Basic to our analysis is an understanding of the concept of 'myth'.

The Concept of Myth

Throughout this book reference is made explicitly, but more often implicitly, to 'myth'. Myth is a second order semiotic system whose function is to distort, but not to make disappear (Barthes, 1973:121). Myth transforms history into nature: dominant historical processes are made to appear 'natural' and 'inevitable', even 'God-given'. Myths do not provide explanations, but invest their expression with a statement of fact: 'blacks in America are different'. This historical 'fact' depoliticises speech and shifts politico-economic issues onto 'cultural' imperatives. Hence, National Party politicians in some of the propaganda films discussed can conclude when defending apartheid, that America is 'two countries' - one white and the other black. The cultural solution for America is apartheid. Since cultural 'differences' are assumed to be the cause of 'friction' between whites and blacks and between blacks and blacks and everybody else, it is a short semantic step to the idea of 'own' cultures in their 'own areas' under their 'own' governments. This logic therefore convincingly argues that the reduction of cultural or intergroup friction can only be **solved** by apartheid - the physical separation of 'the races'. This logic is legitimised through myth. According to Roland Barthes:

myth consists in overturning culture into nature or, at least, the social and cultural, the ideological, the historical into the 'natural'. What is nothing but a product of class division and its moral, cultural and aesthetic consequences is presented (stated) as being a 'matter of course'; under mythical inversion, the quite contingent foundations of the utterance become Common Sense, Right Reason, the Norm, General Opinion ... (Barthes, 1973:165).

Barthes' statement could be applied to most of the films explored in this project. Just as the state propaganda films try to mystify history - as in **A Place Called Soweto** - 'naturalising' the official historical record in terms of dominant Afrikaner perspectives - so the British series on **The White Tribe of Africa** is a little more than a product of the liberal moral values - the Western 'Norm' - of a guilt-ridden British public on the consequences of their earlier colonisation of Africa. Just as myths depoliticise speech, both liberal and apartheid myths de-economise causation. Pro-apartheid films never mention the exploitative racial-capitalist basis of apartheid; and many critical films like **The White Tribe of Africa** simply ignore the imperatives of international, and particularly British capital, on the original formation of apartheid structures from the eighteenth century to the present day.

Myths change. The stories by which a culture explains or makes sense of some aspect of reality are dynamic. They change, and can change rapidly in order to meet the evolving needs and values of the culture of which they are part (Fiske, 1982:93). This is particularly evident in the portrayal of the 'Bushmen' by white film-makers. From uncivilised savages in early films, they are now romanticised and shown to be pawns caught up in the destructive web that calls itself civilisation.

Our point is that the ruling classes, the hegemonic bloc, propagate myths about other classes and groups precisely because they have political control: they are the myth-makers. They create and modify various myths to suit the political exigencies of the moment. The mediation is **one-way:** whites own the means of production and the means of communication. Therefore, only whites are able to portray how the 'races' see 'each other'.

Paradoxically, this one-way perspective is then labelled 'cross-cultural communication'. Because blacks are seen on the screen, the assumption is made that blacks are therefore 'communicating' their perspectives and values.

The situation would be little different if the state allowed the working class, the dispossessed or 'blacks' in general to make films about themselves (**of** cultures as Sol Worth would say) as a way of obviating the propagation of false myths. This would result in a sophisticated ventriloquism: we'd have the government endorsed homeland 'leaders' and so-called community councillors talking about 'our people', 'ons mense', 'die bruin mense', 'the Xhosa nation', 'the Zulus', etc., thus reflecting the 'General Opinion' or 'Common Sense' legitimised in the dominant white discourse by means of 'mythical inversion'. In any case, there is not a single ethnographic production in South Africa where a film with an ethnographic purpose has been made entirely by subordinate groups or classes. Films are made **about** them by whites. This immediately determines that South Africans perceive each other from only one point of view - the 'Common Sense' one - on celluloid at the moment. Even if the subordinate groups were allowed access to the means of communication and exhibition, their messages would probably be considered subversive and so removed from the screen through censorship and other means. In other words, unless such media producing groups adopt the dominant discourse - the 'Right Reason' - of the state politico-semantic framework (exemplified by, for instance, 'intergroup relations', 'co-responsibility', 'negotiation', etc.), it is unlikely that they will be given an adequate hearing by the state, or their arguments accorded any logical or political - let alone, ethnographic - validity. Witness the continuing harrassment of oppositional film and video producers, cultural and media workers (Tomaselli, 1985).

A fundamental element in myth-making is access to and control of the mass media through which these myths - and language - can be propagated. In fact, the dominant classes would be acting against their class interests if they did not propagate myths about the groups and classes they hold in subordination.

It is to an analysis of the myth-making processes and how they can be subverted in film and video that this book is aimed.

CHAPTER 2

ETHNOGRAPHIC FILM : A THEORETICAL OVERVIEW

INTRODUCTION

The South African political discourse of the 1980s roots itself in absolutes - facts, objectiveness and the "hard, tangible and exploitable images of reality" (Steyn, 1981) - but paradoxically, it also implies **degrees of fact:** fact, true facts and hard facts. This semantic contradiction hides a welter of political machination as language and other forms of expression locate the site of struggle between dominant and opposing ideologies.

Realities change because priorities - economic, social and political - change. Nothing is absolute, not even 'exact sciences' like physics. Einstein's principle of relativity terminated the assumption that objectivity could be taken for granted. There is no 'God's-eye' point of view without human mediation. Time and space exist only as they are observed by someone at some point in time and from some point in space. They have meaning not as absolute quantities but are relative to other observations from other points in space at other points in time.

The loss of absolutes in science seems, however, to have had little effect on the reliance on absolutes in some areas of social science. This is because political positions require leaps of faith into selfcontained dimensions of ideological logic. Faiths **are** absolute. They **are** objective. They **are** real. From this vantage point, oppositional images **are** defective. This can be 'proved' through the construction of certain positivist methods which take ideological assumptions for granted. Applied in the field, they more often than not support the hypothesis and prove points which are then taken as fact. Bill Nichols points out the crudity of this assumption:

we should be aware that the world of visual sense impressions does not constitute irrefutable evidence for a given set of statements. The evidence itself must be constituted and, with it, the facts we sometimes think are 'out there' in the visible world. Were it otherwise, presumably there would be a finite number of facts that one, and only one, theory would organise with maximum accuracy, consistency, simplicity and explanatory power (Nichols, 1981:262).

What naïve positivist methods, often clouded by an indiscriminate use of numerical techniques - and politically neutralised as 'scientific' - do not take into account, are cultural myths which inform a society's deployment of language, whether social or scientific (see, e.g. Le Grange, 1980). The 'God's-eye view' informs these myths and reality is defined (albeit unconsciously) in terms of absolutes. A new battle then occurs around the new signs of communication as the positivists try to defend their pronouncement of reality against 'subversives': Marxist-based scholars and others. By labelling historically-oriented paradigms which proceed from the economic as anti-Christian, the 'political' positivists are able to denegrate legitimate activity in terms of religious and scientific discourse (see, e.g. Steyn, 1981). In any case, this theologically-derived form of naïve positivism is trapped within its own incestuousness. The 'God's-eye view' approach is determinate. It denies alternatives, other ways of seeing things. It hides relationships and invisible connections. Surface appearances become paramount, and reality becomes literal and defined in terms of what information is available to the senses. The hidden dimensions recede further into the darkness. Only the points of light, the fragmented pieces of 'reality' are noticed. These are studied in isolation of each other. The connections are not seen or even searched out. Relativity becomes irrelevant.

Science is not a given, there are no "rules for inducing correct theories from fact" (Kuhn, 1977:279). In other words, science constitutes its own object. In the context of this study that object is ethnographic film - an imaginative posit (Popper, 1963) - evolved by anthropologist film-makers for empirical application.

DOCUMENTARY, ETHNOGRAPHY AND 'THE IMPRESSION OF REALITY'

Despite the rich potential in South Africa for the production and study of documentary and ethnographic film, this country has lagged behind developments elsewhere, not only in theoretical discussion but the finished product as well. The few critical analyses which have been done on this area of South African film (Van Zyl, 1980a; Tomaselli, 1980a) show up a paucity of ethnographic understanding of the films under review, and very often, a deliberate ideological distortion in favour of the myths held by the dominant culture. Examples range from the many early films on the !Kung, all very similar in content, treatment and ideological perspective, to the blatant manipulation of images and sounds in documentaries designed to give a favourable impression of South Africa and its apartheid policy.

A visual analysis suggests a confusion of styles and techniques where some propaganda documentaries masquerade as ethnography while overtly ethnographic films tend to lack technical sophistication and competent craft skills. Most of these productions also lack a clear expression of the epistemological principles which underlie their construction. Indeed, the variety of approaches, intentions and purposes manifested in those films that have been made suggests that an urgent appraisal of the attributes of ethnographic film is necessary.

DOCUMENTARY FILM, ETHNOGRAPHIC FILM THEORY

Traditionally, ethnography has been concerned with the collection and recording of data about societies and their cultures. The analysis and theoretical interpretation of such data is the domain of anthropology. The concept of ethnographic film, however, is fraught with conceptual difficulties, opposing schools of thought and interdisciplinary rivalry between anthropologists, visual anthropologists, ethnographers, sociologists and not least, film-makers and film-theoreticians. We need to examine some of these approaches before defining our own position.

The Pluralist View

A pluralistic position is taken by Karl Heider (1972:1) who argues that "It is probably best not to try to define ethnographic films. In the broadest sense, most films are ethnographic - that is, if "we take 'ethnographic' to mean 'about people'". This approach is supported by Walter Goldschmidt's (1972) more specific definition: "Ethnographic film is film which endeavours to interpret the behaviour of people of one culture by using shots of people doing precisely what they would have been doing if the cameras were not present".

Sol Worth's (1981:75) semiotic-based definition is more sophisticated, defining ethnographic film as a method "by means of which we can study the signs, and the rules of implication and inference, that we employ when we use those signs in films that are intended to describe and present the customs and ways of people all over the world". All these definitions reflect the paradoxical nature of the emerging discipline. Bill Nichols (1981:238) points to remaining difficulties:

> Most often ethnographic films attempt to explain or describe some aspect of another culture to members of the film-maker's own culture within a context informed to a varying extent by traditional anthropological and ethnographic concerns and concepts and perpetuating most of their political limitations: ideology is a word seldom used in studies of other cultures, and considerations of who defines culture and how (where do We draw the line around Them?) or, even more, of the ideological implications of representing one culture to another receive scant attention. These limitations contribute, I suspect, to the generally ill-defined nature of this whole enterprise. They certainly help account for much of the difficulty we encounter when trying to place films that only partially place themselves. Even the loose thematic definition adopted here poses a number of problems ... but no better alternative seems possible.

Here, Nichols is drawing a distinction between **analysis** of films from an ethnographic point of view, and the making of films from the raw material of life which is the style of documentary. This is a crucial distinction which we will develop later when showing how analysis of existing films can point to the development of cinematic techniques which can be applied in the field.

The Exclusivist View

Propounded by Jay Ruby (1971, 1975, 1976, 1977) in opposition to Heider's broad approach, the exclusivist view denies the ethnographic validity of the above and draws a distinction between films which are "anthropologically useful" and those which meet the more rigorous criteria of a "filmic ethnography". The crux of this distinction rests with the **intention** of the film-maker. That is to say, "While all films are potentially useful to anthropologists, that does not necessarily mean that these films should be labelled as ethnography" (Ruby, 1975:106), since they do not conform to the critical criteria derived from the tradition of anthropology.

In contrast to Heider, Ruby (1975:105) argues that "ethnography is about culture which does **include** people, but in a special context that differs from the way biologists, painters, or psychologists deal with people".

Ruby concludes that the stance taken by Heider and Goldschmidt loses it specificity in its all-inclusiveness and that anyone in their terms, regardless of training and method, is able to 'do ethnography'.

Photographs, films and video are a common research tool in anthropology, but have been underutilised within the tradition of written anthropology. Film cannot, however, be regarded as ethnography analogous to written anthropology because the two modes are informed by quite different scientific methods, practices and codes.

Following Worth and Adair (1972), Ruby (1975) classifies all footage as potentially anthropologically useful in so far as it displays information about the culture of both the film-maker and subject. In contrast to Heider, this is not a bland assertion that all film is ethnographic but potentially ethnographic depending on the uses to which it is put. For a film to qualify as ethnography it has to conform to rigorous scientific criteria. Ethnographic film-makers thus have a primary obligation to the tradition of anthropology, both in investigation and presentation.

The starting point for a filmic ethnography, according to Ruby (1975), is the transposition of certain basic criteria of written ethnography onto film. First, ethnography must describe a **whole** culture, or a unit of that culture (e.g. a ritual). Second, ethnography should be informed by a theory around which the data is organised and assigned priority. Third, ethnography must reveal methodology (reflexivity). Fourth, it must contain a specific linguistic lexicon for written work. It would appear that Ruby is thereby also calling for a specific filmic lexicon where cinematic signs and codes are analogous to the discourse of written anthropology. This semiotic qualification is difficult to apply to film as "We do not have a lexicon of images, as we do of words, by which we may check on a culturally agreed upon signification" (Worth, 1981: 75).

FILMIC ETHNOGRAPHY VERSUS THE PLURALIST VIEW

A consideration of Heider's work cannot be done in isolation from the contrary views of Ruby, MacDougall and Nichols. Heider's pluralist view argues against a strict definition of ethnographic film. All films, he claims, are about people. While films like **The Tribal Identity** or **Ghandi** may not subscribe to Goldschmidt's open ended definition, they are nevertheless 'about people' and would at least expose some elements of the filmmaker's own culture. Nichols' (1981:238) rider, that ethnographic films deal primarily with the question of 'what to do with people' is crucial in identifying documents of actuality from docu-dramas, structured documentary and fiction. A further distinction is provided by MacDougall (1978) who, apart from fleshing out fundamental differences between the written word and film, suggests that a distinction be drawn between "ethnographic footage" and "ethnographic films". 'Footage' serves primarily as an anthropological aid in its unedited form and does not claim to be anything more than that. Local examples would include the unedited footage of indigenous healers shot by Gerard Schutte in Venda, and the material recorded by Len Holdstock and Keyan Tomaselli in Soweto.

Although both Ruby and MacDougall suggest new directions for the use of ethnographic film, neither develop their alternatives. Where MacDougall calls for a new paradigm, Ruby places his trust in written ethnography. Unlike Heider, however, he does not owe uncritical allegiance to the written method and explores the possibilities of a comparative analysis between the two media.

The remainder of this chapter will not be concerned with written anthropology **per se,** but will focus attention on questions of ideology and distinctions between textual analysis on the one hand and production on the other.

A COMPOSITE APPROACH

While both Ruby and Heider have identified pertinent elements of ethnographic film, they do not offer explicit semiotic/production strategies which could inform the foundation of an ethnographic film practice. Nichols' key question of 'what to do with people' takes on a semiotic specificity in the task of "how to erect both a film form and a film theory within the paradoxical space of the relationship between the indexical sign and referent" (Nichols, 1981:283). This chapter will attempt to explore these ideas in relation to films made about people in South Africa. A definition of ethnographic film as applied in this study will emerge from this theoretical exploration.

Form and Reflexivity

Ruby (1975:108) criticises contemporary ethnographic film-makers for uncritically adopting a "set of artistic and humanistic ideas derived from documentary film ... (they) assume documentary film conventions are the most suitable conventions for this purpose".

The documentary style lays a heavy emphasis on narration as a means of supporting the visual content. Methodology, however, is significantly absent from this form of film-making. Ruby concludes that this lack would be a serious omission in a filmic ethnography which should include a scientific justification for the multitude of decisions made by the crew during the production process. Unless the film-maker is willing to subject these decisions to scientific scrutiny, "then it is difficult, if not impossible, to justify or think of the film in a scientific context" (Ruby, 1971).

Although Ruby has little to say about technique and its ideological determinants, and how content is at the mercy of electronic and machine processes, he does have some important points to make about the production process. He believes that film-makers, along with anthropologists, have an ethical, political, aesthetic and scientific obligation to be reflexive and self-critical. The basis of Ruby's (1977) philosophy is the equation Producer-Process-Product, borrowed from anthropologist Johannes Fabian (1971). Most film-makers, argues Ruby, present audiences with Product, but not an exposition of the Producer-Process element. His criticism of documentaries is that they are produced in an effort to be unbiased or objective. According to conventional documentarists, there is no need to reveal Process because it would be interpreted as unnecessarily personal, self-indulgent or, because it would have the effect of jolting the viewer out of the film's continuity which denies the presence of the crew.

The 'objective' documentarists would argue that the form of documentary governs the parameters of production and treatment of subject matter. There would thus be no need to expose methodology because viewer expectations are being fulfilled by the form. This assertion takes for granted a direct relationship between the pro-filmic and filmic events and is based on the premise of an objective world-out-there where 'truth' can be found by the anthropologist and documentarist. This form of filmic positivism takes no account of the production process whereby film-makers **impose** meaning on the world, thus creating the kind of truth consistent with the dominant perspectives of their culture. Ruby concludes that unless the Producer-Process in **conjunction** with the Product is revealed, a critical and sophisticated understanding of the Product is impossible.

The concept of reflexivity provides one method of combining the Producer-Process-Product relationships into the text of a film in a way which will make audiences aware of the processes employed by film-makers to shape their interpretations:

> Being reflexive means that the producer deliberately and intentionally reveals to his audience the underlying epistemological assumptions which caused him to formulate a set of questions in a particular way, to seek answers to these questions in a particular way and finally to present his findings in a particular way (Ruby, 1977:4).

MacDougall (1975) emphasises the subject rather than the text. He suggested various ways of recording the subjects responses to the film after viewing it, and the extent to which they relate their own experiences of how their participation affected their own experience. The objective is to break down the mysticism that surrounds the film-maker's authority over the production process so common in conventional film production. Timothy Ache's **Axe Fight** about Yanomamö social conflict is the film which most successfully employs MacDougall's proposition, and Ruby's thoughts about reflexivity. No less than three alternative versions of the film showing unedited footage, structured explanation and final edited product are provided. The overall effect is to lay bare the evidence and methodology for independent scrutiny.

While Ruby's arguments are consistent with Heider's position of exposing methodology, it is inconsistent with Sol Worth's ethnographic semiotics which shifts attention from films about cultures to films of cultures.

Films of Cultures

The repositioning of film within anthropology drawing on a linguistically-based semiology resulted from the work of Sol Worth (1972: 1981). He took Malinowski's (1922:25) research dictum quite literally: "grasping the native's point of view, his relation to life, to realise his vision of his world". Worth acknowledged that no matter what precautions the ethnographer took, a cultural transference would inevitably be encoded into the film. Reflexivity was not, therefore, an intrinsic element of Worth's praxis. Most ethnographic film made by the observing culture had therefore to be classified as film **about** rather than **of** culture. The distinction is fundamental. The former is superficial, selective and conducted in terms of the film-maker's own culture rather than with what the subject culture has to tell. In other words, the parameters of study are governed by what the anthropologist or film-maker's culture needs to know. By accepting the premise that films about people intentionally or unintentionally encode the values of the film-maker's own culture, then it would be logical to reverse the process and allow the subject culture or group to make films about themselves. Such material could then be treated as raw data by the ethnographer. Worth believed that scholars needed to adopt a methodology and theory which would enable ethnographic film-makers to make inferences on the subject film-maker's **intent.** In other words, Worth argued that the way a subject group edited the basic building blocks of film (or Eisenstein's 'shot') would parallel their world view.

The filmic units of Worth's visual analogue to linguistics - vidistics - were the camera shot, the **cademe,** and the editing shot, the **edeme,** which are then combined into the syntagma. The application of this theory, he hoped, would identify universal transcultural rules for the shaping and sharing of meanings in film. The evidence for this hypothesis was gathered from the study he conducted with a group of Navajo Indians with anthropologist John

Adair (1972).   This project sought to identify dimensions of cogni-
tion and social values hidden from verbal discourse, especially
when "it is done in the language of the investigator" (Worth and
Adair, 1972:11).   The Navajo project supported Worth's hypothesis
that the subject culture may see their world very differently from
the way the anthropologist may describe it.   However, the problems of measurement still remain. Not only does the differential
access to the film medium and its technology constitute an inequable power relationship between those who study and those who
are being studied, but in teaching people film-making, we implicitly teach them what and how to film.   As Worth (1981:19) states,
"The use of a mode of communication is not easily separable from
the scientific codes and rules about the content of that mode".
While accepting that technology carried with it "our codes, our
mythic and narrative forms", he felt that these could be neutralised by informing the subject culture that film cameras **need not**
be used only in the ways of the ... societies that introduce them"
(Worth, 1981:19).

The 'Us' 'Them' Dichotomy: Where do We Draw the line around Them?

While the discipline of anthropology assumes the primacy of social
scientists in their interactions with subjects, ethnography becomes
a one-way flow of specific information governed by the parameters of the anthropologist's culture. The material (both written
and filmed) gathered, therefore, inevitably serves to illustrate
rather than govern ethnographic enquiry. The filmic consideration
of culture reverses the use of film as merely a recording device
to one which is both documenter **and** medium capable of being
employed as a research tool **combined** with the subject culture de-
termining the parameters of study by encoding their own cultural
values and norms on film themselves.   This would reverse the
one-way flow of information and reduce the degree of cultural imposition on the part of the ethnographer.

The subject-intention oriented approach proposed by Worth is re-
volutionary as far as anthropology is concerned. Instead of the
anthropologist being dominant in the process of investigation (per-
sonified in the idea of the 'expert' field worker embarking on a

study of 'other' cultures), Worth argues that anthropologists need, and have a responsibility, to encourage a mode of self-expression which can serve as a cultural artifact worthy of study. This requires a two-fold change of methodological direction. First, subjects have to be taught to articulate their values and cognitive processes in a new visual form. Second, and far more problematic is the need to re-orient the discipline of anthropology (and structures of film distribution and exhibition) to enable it to accommodate a subject-oriented worldview encoded on film.

A subject-oriented reflexive paradigm would go some way to resolving criticism of a one-way information flow. Remaining criticisms could be engaged through an analysis of purpose, also central to Worth's theories.

Purpose

Related to the idea of intention is the question of purpose. Because Worth regarded even 'completed' films as raw data, he was able to discredit definitions which classified film as ethnographic in terms of their content. He counter argued that films became ethnographic in terms of the **use** to which they are put: "in order to know something about ethnographic films, we need to examine not the films, but why they are made and how they are used" (Worth, 1981:76). In other words, we need to study the relationship between the film code and its context. In a country like South Africa where culture has become grossly politicised through apartheid ideology, this question becomes crucial. Films used for ethnographic purposes in the classroom may well become political weapons in other transmission-distributive contexts.

Worth's foregrounding of purpose balances Ruby's Producer-Process-Product schema which remains incomplete without reference to an Audience. It is, after all, the audience (or interpreter) that has to make sense (or produce interpretants) of the signified intentions of the film-maker. Viewers act out different social practices, each of which confer different and even contradictory contexts which will determine the direction and closure of semiosis. In other words, different audiences bring different codes to bear on the text. The anthropologist will tend to react more in terms of denotative overcoding, while the mass audience may respond more to connotative undercodes in terms of the ideological perspectives. This often leads to aberrant decoding where the addressee receives an idiosyncratic message. A viewing of **The Tribal Identity** on television, for example, identifies the viewer as a recipient of 'entertainment', but shown in a classroom the interpreter becomes more critical in terms of his/her knowledge of written anthropology. Its screening in the South African embassy in a foreign country would tend to place it as a political series justifying the prevailing social and political organisation of the country. (This extracoding of interpretants will be re-examined with reference to differing audience responses to **On Becoming a Sangoma** later in this chapter.)

Thus far we have established that ethnographic film-making tends to occur within a power relationship where interpretations are based, not on the parameters of the observed culture, but from the perspectives of the observer. This relationship may be more accurately defined in terms of ideology and perceptions of truth. The two concepts are linked and are complicated by the positivist notions of both film-makers and anthropologists.

DOCUMENTARY AND THE 'IMPRESSION OF REALITY'

The debate about realism in the cinema hinges on the opposition between 'mere appearances', the reality of things as we perceive them, and the essential truth of 'true reality', one which is not normally seen or perceived. This section will endeavour to examine the elements of cinematic truth within the tenets of film theory.

Theories of realist cinema demonstrate an overwhelming concern with the concept of truth. These theories have been evolved in close association with film-directors operating in the field who have developed a whole range of styles and treatments which are often categorised under the banner of documentary.

John Grierson, who was the first to rigorously apply the term 'documentary' to a particular kind of film, argued that "Documentary would photograph the living scene and the living story" (Williams, 1980:17). One of Grierson's more ideologically sensitive colleagues, Paul Rotha (1936:113-4) stated that "Documentary's essence lies in the dramatization of actual material". Further, he suggested that

"Documentary must be the voice of the people speaking from the homes and factories and field of the people" (Rotha, 1936:128) and that film is "not mere recorded description" (Rotha, 1936:83).

Paradoxically, both realism and anti-realist theories are committed to the idea of 'truth'. Williams and Nichols, however, tend to interchange the terms 'documentary' and 'realism', suggesting connections where previous theorists sought discrete categories. The growing theoretical shift back to the study of documentary, which is now taking on a more general description, is partly a reflection of the desire to use film for scientific rather than merely socio-political purposes. Hence the concern for scientific accuracy and the need to examine more closely the semiotic properties of 'the actual' referred to by Rotha and Grierson.

Reality: The struggle for the sign

Individuals make sense of reality through semiotic systems. The different ways they make sense of it identifies one culture from another (Muller, 1983). These are not God given, but largely a response to environmental, social, political and economic conditions. Culture is taken to be that ensemble of social practices through which defined groups within classes express themselves in unique ways which enable them to better cope with their material circumstances (Tomaselli, 1983b). Different classes, though often from the same cultural background, have different experiences which they internalise into 'common sense' (Tomaselli, Tomaselli and Muller, 1986). The different classes thus 'see' life differently. These varying perceptions arise out of the economic relations of production and often lead to ideological conflict.

The conflict comes about through an economic struggle (the class struggle) which, in modern society, often manifests itself on a large scale within the media. In other words, the commercial media are used by economically and politically powerful interests within the state to support the capitalist relations of production and to legitimise the social, economic and political organisation of society (Hall **et al,** 1978; Miliband, 1973; Therborn, 1980; Bozzoli, 1981; Tomaselli, Tomaselli and Muller, 1986). The media thus accredit a dominant economic reality over a subordinate one.

Perception of the world is not direct or unmediated. Individuals and societies encounter the world through signs and semiotic representations. The way their signs are organised create codes of interpretation. Thus different codes can give differing interpretations of the same event or thing. Particular sets of coded meaning are the essence of ideological and cultural discourses relative to class experience. Codes are, therefore, historically based. They are not natural, neutral or even necessary. They are, however, taken for granted by the dominant ideology, and legitimised as natural occurrences or 'timeless truths' - the 'God's-eye view'. They are presented as 'common sense' (as seen in **White Roots in Africa**), the unquestioned way of interpreting reality (as in **South African Mosaic**) or doing things (as in **A Place Called Soweto**). Deviant interpretations (e.g. **This We Can Do for Justice and Peace**) are accused of 'bias' (Appeal Board, Case No. 155/81). Bias, however, suggests that there must be a quality of 'non-bias', and that by merely 'cracking the code', one can identify truth or reality. Cracking the code and discovering causation is a complex process for it involves penetrating the naturalness of common sense and examining the cultural and historical form of the code.

If ideology accounts for the 'lived' relations between people and their world (Althusser, 1971:233), then we must accept that meaning is saturated with the ideological imperatives of society. Ideology is the code of representations (Eco in Heck, 1980) through which we are able to build up a picture of the world around us. Although meaning embodied in this code may seem self-evident, this does not mean that it is a direct reflection of actual conditions. In nearly every case, the conditions we 'see' through decoding the signs contained in the code are only **imaginary**. Despite this, the code has the force of an objective reality and individuals then assume that their 'reality' is the only valid one, and that it is a fixed set of immutable laws which cannot be questioned.

Ideology - and hence reality - does not exist 'out there' - but is rather a set of semantic rules:

> Ideology is not a particular type of message, or a class of social discourses, but it is one of the many levels or organization of the messages, from the point of view of its semantic properties. Ideology is therefore a **level of signification**

which can be present in any type of message, even in the scientific discourse. Any material of social communication is susceptible to **ideological reading** (Veron in Heck, 1980:123).

Dominant codes and meanings are not invulnerable. They are susceptible to aberrant decoding, co-option, persuasion and can be overthrown. **The media are a prime site of struggle for the sign.** The ideological struggle is also a struggle for meaning. Therefore, at its most basic level, the struggle is for the sign (Tomaselli **et al**, 1986). (See Chapter 5 on the discussion of **To Act a Lie, White Roots in Africa** and **A Place Called Soweto**.) Where counter ideological or alternative discourses have little access to the commercial media, they develop their own channels through oppositional networks (e.g. BBC-TV, UNESCO, local media organizations and so on). Social struggle is simultaneously a struggle for political power through the struggle for the sign.

We may now return to the question of the 'actual' and its relation to documentary film. Extrapolating the above discussion, we may define documentary as a code which organises messages in a particular way. It is a system of semantic rules in terms of content ('actuality'), the semiotic rules of structuring and paradigmatic selection. What is not said - the structured absences - is part of the message as the absence of alternative - or oppositional paradigms - is as much part of the plane of content as is what is present in the plane of signification (the denotative).

The Distinction Between Ethnographic Film and Documentary

What separates ethnographic film from documentary hinges on iconic signs and the word 'actual', and how much of this undercoded quality remains once the film has been treated 'creatively', 'aesthetically' or 'dramatically' in order to make a movie acceptable to entertainment conditioned audiences. (Anthropologists, of course, lie outside this practice.) Various realist styles allowing extracoding activity have been evolved to meet this need: the films of the reality directors, cinéma vérité, camera-stylo and neo-realism through to the more conscious documentary styles with a social and political purpose such as Kino-Eye, and political documentary **per se**. According to Andre Bazin, a notable theorist of cinematic realism involving the first four styles mentioned, they record "what happens" (Bazin, 1967:158-9). He is unconcerned that these styles, as indeed all cinematic expression, interpret reality through the processes and codes of camera optics, framing, editing, chemical treatment, and very often, the post synchronisation of sound effects and music. Overlaid on these influences are the productive forces and ideology of the film-makers themselves.

To approach an aesthetic treatment of the 'actual' through any of these styles ultimately devolves upon a hierarchy of 'truth' where the reality portrayed is relative to the technology of the cinematic apparatus, the techniques of production, and the objectives, attitudes and ideology of the film-maker. In other words, despite its **apparent** realism, film is not neutral or objective. This is what makes the study of film so difficult. Christian Metz puts it this way: "A film is so difficult to explain because it is so easy to understand" (Monaco, 1981:130). Unlike written language, the short-circuited nature of the cinematic sign collapses the signifier into the signified presenting not an easily identified sign system - like words - but an apparent **absence** of such a system. It is this spurious realism which leads the audience to take the image and its combinational syntagma for granted: what is shown must be what there is. Acceptance of this surface reality coincides with the viewers own interpretation of the world which they share with others of their class and culture. In this respect, Paul Rotha (1936:134) observed that "most documentary is only truthful in that it represents an attitude of mind". Like religion and morals, film cannot be considered apart from the materialist trappings of society (Rotha, 1936:62).

A distinction needs to be made between 'realistic' and 'realism'. A documentary may be realistic in its concern with the iconicity of actuality, but 'realism' applies not only to the material, but more especially to the method of approach to that material (Rotha, 1936:135) at an indexical level which creates an apparent space-time continuity. Thus, films can only be understood through an understanding of their styles.

Grierson's democratic idealism blinded him to the role of the economy in capitalist society and cinema's relation to it, and on a broader level, the state. Grierson never considered the state as part of the class system. He saw the political and economic situation as being dependent upon the policies of the party in power, rather than as a structural process supported by the whole hegemonic bloc. Unlike his Russian counterparts, therefore, he made the entirely false distinction between the state and the party in power.

Normally, anthropologists work outside the formal state system, at institutions of higher learning. As such, their practice is usually self-contained and uninterfered with by the state. However, where anthropologists are employed by the state to make films or are contracted by para-statal bodies such as the Television Service of the South African Broadcasting Corporation (SABC-TV), they will find themselves drawn into the consensual signifying practices of such communications institutions. Whatever scientific, informational or ethnographic intentions the film-maker may have started with, will inevitably be modified in terms of the consensual discourse of the institution, itself embedded within the ruling hegemony. Where anthropologists like Peter Becker (who directed **The Tribal Identity**) saw little tension between his ethnographic objectives and the propaganda imperatives of the SABC, his cameraman, Lionel Friedberg, negotiated the consensual discourse in a far more discursive manner in the later series that he shot and directed, **They Came From the East.** Despite the relative autonomy he won on this series (see Chapter 3), he was unable to sustain the same degree of independence after the first episode of **And Then Came The English,** from which he resigned as director after interference from both the SABC and his employer.

Conservative institutional responses are contributing factors to the 'impression of reality'. The context of production very often forces a specific signifying perspective. Depending on the relationship of the film-maker/company to the state, or what Althusser (1971) calls an Ideological State Apparatus (such as the SABC), the film-maker is relatively free (or not free) to make use of extracoding functions. Where the academic is responsible only to the academic community, the documentarist is tied in terms of institutional constraints. The struggle for the sign thus occurs at the intersection of the state, the economy and political practice.

Technology and Distortion

On a technical level, little attention has been given to the unique semiotic properties found within the various media. A clear distinction needs to be made between film on the one hand and video on the other. Their dissimilar semiotic and technological qualities have serious implications for the reproduction of images for they distort and manipulate 'the impression of reality' in quite different ways. The signs of these two media are also argued to be differently perceived (see Merrelyn and Emery, 1980; Venis, 1980: and Balachoff, 1981).

Technology, in turn, is dependent upon the relations of production (Williams, 1974). The development of the cinematic apparatus and the kinds of images it records, in the West at least, are subject to capitalist forces of production. Economic exchange relations separate art films, commercial films and sponsored documentary from ethnographic productions which are made outside the market economy. Film and art in general are a contribution to a definite period in history, and styles, philosophies, techniques, ideology and interpretations can all be traced back to their material sources in the way that the host society has ordered its relations of production. Film-makers all too readily accept the 'ready to wear' set of conventions handed to them by the manufacturers whose equipment is usually designed to work within conventional practice which isolates process from form and content.

The Integration of Form, Process and Content in Ethnographic Film

Many film-makers have a limited understanding of their subject and how it should be filmed. This is evident in many of the early films made about the !Kung. The relationship between film-makers and their subject matter will remain problematical where the film-maker has no implicit or explicit understanding of semiotics or documentary or ethnographic film theories. Examples of this dislocation are the films of Andrew Tracey and Gei Zantzinger on African music (e.g. **The Chopi Timbila Dance** and a number from the **Mbira Series).** On the one hand these films are clearly explanatory of indigenous musical techniques, but on the other, tend to be packed with technical clichés, an unmotivated and confusing overuse of optical effects (e.g. dissolves in **Ndando Yawusiwana** made by Zantzinger), an over-reliance on the sound track for information, incompetent camera work and a distressing lack of understanding between form and content. The resulting films lack conceptual clarity, clearly articulated signifiers (e.g. the use of dissolves to suggest the transition of time rather than merely for 'aesthetic effect'), and tend to be divorced from their contexts. It is only due to the musical knowledge of Tracey that these films have any merit at all.

Some experiments have been conducted on how best to present ethnographic material, particularly where the film-maker is not always aware of what is happening. One recalls **Axe Fight** which documents familial conflict involving three lineages in a Yanoma-ṁo village in South America (see Asch, 1975). It was made without preparation or initial understanding of what was happening. The film was put together in three different ways. The first was the cutting together of the unedited footage (the cademes). This version, which does not interpret, shows up the difficulties facing the crew whose comments and discussion about what they thought was happening is recorded on the sound track. The second version, a slow motion replay, offers an explanation through hindsight. It identifies the combatants and accounts for their behaviour. A lineage chart delineates the conflict in terms of marriage and descent. Explanation is assisted through editing intervention through the use of freeze frames, graphics, slow motion and descriptive narration. A third edited version is descriptive, lacking the elaborated codes of anthropological discourse. In watching the three versions, it becomes immediately apparent how much prior knowledge is required to interpret the relationships which are governing the action and to answer the question 'what is really happening here?'. In this case, explanation came after the event. The film could not have been shown in its first version without being integrated into a lecture or a sequence in a longer film dealing with the intersection of politics and religion and the concomitant ritual that helps bind small groups together (Asch, 1975:388).

In South Africa, **On Becoming a Sangoma** was made under similar circumstances, although the events which took place were far more predictable - only the details of the ritual differed in relation to other enactments celebrating the same events (**Twasa** graduation and homecoming). While both director and cameraman knew more or less the course that events would take, they did not know why things happened as they did in the detail they would have liked. As with **Axe Fight**, explanation was sought after the cademes had been linked together, this time from the subjects (the **sangomas**) themselves who were shown the film. Narration was kept to a minimum and no attempt was made to edit the film according to conventional principles.

The two examples discussed above suggest that even ethnographic film which consciously tries to differentiate technique from content making content primary, recorded in terms of specific scientific principles, is subject to distortion. Ethnographic film, however, should be aware of its warping effect through its epistemological principles deriving from both anthropology, and film theory and practice. As vexed as things are, Edgar Morin's (1962) statement is apt: "Truth is not a Holy Grail to be won: it is a shuttle which moves ceaselessly between the observer and the observed, between science and reality".

The next section will tie up some of the above ideas. It will argue that by adhering to certain principles during production incorrect anthropological interpretations can be minimised.

ETHNOGRAPHIC PRODUCTION PRINCIPLES

The adherence to certain production principles during production will help to minimise the displacement of the pro-filmic event resultant upon the technological and semiotic properties of the medium. These principles can also be applied to the analysis of existing films which are not necessarily made from an ethnographic point of view, but which may be 'anthropologically useful'.

HOLISM

All the scholars discussed above place particular emphasis on the notion of holism. Heider (1972), for example, argues that events and rituals must be understood within their social and cultural contexts - whole people in whole acts - is far more significant than more aesthetically pleasing close-ups and fragmented and fleeting behaviour of people and their environment. This principle is designed to prevent a fractured understanding of the pro-filmic event.

The phrase 'whole people in whole acts' should not be read literally for it is the **relation** of 'people' and 'acts' to social and cultural contexts that is important. At this level, film-makers have to extend their field of significations to identify, not merely people and acts at the iconic level, but the indexical and symbolic relations which govern social action. Holism does not mean that the entire film should be shot in wide angle, but that where mid shots, close-ups, etc. are used, they should signify indexical and symbolic specificity. One may move, for example, from the maiming of the sacrificial cow in wide shot to a close-up of the recently quivering flesh which continues to be inhabited by the spirits (see **On Becoming a Sangoma**). The indexical connection between 'quivering flesh' and 'spirits' is established in relation to the **context** of homecoming which is shown by going back to a wide shot to reveal the social interaction going on around the dead cow, and to identify the relationship of the actors with it and the spirits which now inhabit it.

By filming the entire ritual in wide angle only the camera sees more than it needs, is not directed to culturally significant acts and indexical relations are not established. Where the film-maker is in doubt, the use of wide angle is probably the safest way of recording, but the sensitive film-maker will intuitively identify relevant patterns and relationships. This brings us to the intrusion of ideology which guides the 'lived' relation between, not only the subjects, but between the film crew and those subjects. Since preliterate societies and cultures stress the emotional, intuitive and integrative modes of thought over the sequential, mathematically oriented processes, the 'lived' relation between film-makers and their subjects is immediately complicated by apparently exclusive logical systems. The cinematic apparatus is a consequence of the latter but is expected to capture the reality of the former.

The ideology of the film crew usually derives from the productive forces which brought that technology about in the first place. To ask such film-makers to alter their previously unquestioned social practice and to transform their raw material into imaged social relations which reflect the practices endemic to the subjects rather than the film-makers, is a difficult task. This is why it so often happens that film-makers unconsciously impose inaccurate and often, completely incorrect, interpretations on events and processes. Academics, exasperated by the unwillingness of production crews to suspend their slavish devotion to 'professionalism' - the way things are done - have responded by becoming film-makers themselves (e.g. Sol Worth and Len Holdstock).

In still other cases, the observers themselves have intuitively made the connections between the social practices of themselves as film-makers and those of their subjects. In **On Becoming a Sangoma,** we tried to 'feel' the situation, to rely more on the emotional logic of the subjects, than on the linear Western approach or written anthropology. In other words, where conventional scientific logic makes use of the 'object', intuitive reasoning guided us in participating in the object (ritual). This is not easy, particularly when the behaviour patterns one is filming are not part of one's own culture. However, once we felt more comfortable with this kind of holistic logic, if only on a conceptual level, it became easier to sense patterns and relationships which were part of the dynamic of the event itself and which radiated outwards from it. This helped the crew (usually Holdstock, myself, an assistant and sometimes an interpreter) to virtually become part of the event in a way which minimised our intrusion. Our disturbance was thus minimal as the event attracted more attention than did the camera. Morin (1962:4) has described this relationship between the observers and the observed as one of "intensive sociality". This occurs where the observers have spent so much time with their subjects that they lose interest in the camera.

Trust is an important element in establishing intensive sociality. In South Africa, film producers have often abused that trust by financially exploiting the people being filmed and by misrepresenting their behaviour to secure saleability of their products. The group of healers who were the subjects of **On Becoming a Sangoma** had already been in contact with Holdstock for a few years and had established a working relationship which was recorded in his earlier video production, **Indigenous Healers of Africa.**

If the crew does not have an intuitive feel for what is being filmed, the result will be a production which emphasises the parts rather than the whole; the context and what the relation of the parts is to the whole will be missed at the indexical and symbolic levels. We need now to examine the effect of the observers and their technology on the behaviour of the people being studied. This is known as the 'ethnographic presence' (Heider, 1972).

THE ETHNOGRAPHIC PRESENCE

People under observation often act and react for the camera rather than behaving as if it were not present. These responses may be as gross as mugging for the camera or as subtle as causing imperceptible changes in clothing so as to eliminate sloppy behaviour. During the shooting of **On Becoming a Sangoma,** for example, while dancing was taking place in a military style tent in the garden of a house in Soweto, the **Sangoma**-teacher instructed all those present to take their shoes off so that they could be closer to the earth. If not, they were told, the white guests would leave as the performance did not meet traditional standards.

The disturbance which the observers bring to an event must, like the distortion of technology, be identified, measured, and, if possible, held semiotically constant. Two procedures are open to film-makers:

1. They can deny the ethnographic presence by editing out shots which reveal camera consciousness or where equipment such as microphones, tape recorders, cables or members of the crew are visible. This technique supposedly offers 'objectivity' and is considered 'professional' by entertainment conditioned directors whose main concern is a commercial slickness rather than a cinematically honest treatment of content. By excluding themselves from the world of their subjects, film-makers also exclude the subjects from the world of film. The position they adopt is therefore a secretive one which, in its insularity, withholds the very openness they ask of their subjects (MacDougall, 1975:118).

2. Film-makers can build their presence into the structure of the film and actually show the effect that their observation is having on the behaviour of the people being filmed.

This is done in much the same way as the first version of **Axe Fight** where the viewer can hear the crew talking on the sound track. Ruby's (1977) concept of reflexivity would further insist that ethnographic method also be described in the film to establish its scientific validity.

While this technique is considered sloppy by most professional film-makers, the ethnographic presence does offer a basis for the measurement of intrusion.

THE ETHNOGRAPHIC PRESENT

Films which record performance rather than directing it have little use for manipulation of 'actors', sets, lighting and so on. However, film-makers often have to recreate an event where rituals have died out or construct facsimiles of objects no longer in existence. This reconstruction is called the ethnographic present (Heider, 1972).

Films which invisibly mix natural and staged action imply some kind of mysticism (Williams, 1980:90). The kind of mysticism generated depends on the ideology which governs the power relationship between the observers and the observed. **Fighting Sticks,** for example, locates this Zulu custom within an Eastern martial arts context. Conversely, unlike early films emphasising the primitiveness of the 'Bushmen', **Rock Art Treasures** paints a romanticised cinematic sculpture which indicates the naturalness of the desert habitat for the !Kung of today. The mix of dramatic codes, documentary conventions, and a detective-type narrative in **Who is Vasco Mutwa** sets up the question of (ethnic) identity using as its point of departure a small black boy who is portrayed as 'different', but paradoxically, a part of the other 'black nations'.

Cheating is an accepted documentary convention which has the effect of naturalising events and situations. It is, therefore, inadmissible in ethnographic film unless acknowledged through narration and/or sub-titles.

FILM TECHNIQUE AND INTERPRETATIONS OF TRUTH

Emphasis on technique, which characterises what documentary has become, results in a quest for continually improved means (Ellul, 1964). The concern for the part by individual technicians often vitiates the content of the whole. The techniques of camera operation, for example, may be considered by the film-maker to be of

more importance than other objectives. The result may be creative photography using zooms, pull focussing, tracking shots and so
on --- all having the effect of obscuring the actual conditions of
existence of the people the film is dealing with (e.g. **There Lies
Your Land, Die Vroue-revolusie** and **Venda: 'n Nuwe Staat).** The
result is a preferred reading of a visually pleasing movie with
little evidence of accuracy, relationship or integrity.

The consequence of the technological quest - the moulding of the
event for the camera - is to perpetuate an event-oriented interpretation. In the case of the 'Bushmen' films (excluding those of
the Marshalls and Van der Post), the ends have more to do with
profit than with information. These films thus have to be understood within the ideological context of their producers and the
field of significations which govern sponsor attitudes. Very often
these films tell the viewer more about the ideology, attitudes and
prejudices of the producers than they do about their subjects. An
analysis of films made about the !Kung by commercial producers
between 1896 and 1950 will show little change in the way this
group is perceived by film-makers, particularly those of South African origin. They reinforce a God's-eye view common sense
which locates the !Kung as 'primitive'.

The silent versions put it thus: "No God, No Morality, No History" (Van Zyl, 1980a:32). The techniques of production, derived
from a capitalist system provided the semiotic links to perceptions
of the real. So crude were many of these films that they did not
portray the !Kung in even 'man versus nature' terms, but as civilization versus savagery, progress versus backwardness and so on.
Where later films show poetic revelation, the former are hard,
sharp and ruthless ideological imposition. Or as Grierson would
have said, 'propaganda with a political meaning rather than propaganda as social information'. The interpretation of the pro-filmic
event is decided by what the director thinks the audience and/or
sponsor wants. It is this endistancing process which determines
the saleability of the film. The 'real' on film is thus a
commercial reality. These films intercept what audiences consider 'obvious': a film about the 'Bushmen' is obviously about the
Bushmen, and nothing else. The diegetic reconstructions have the
appearance of documentary, but the kind of textual closure that
occurs can only take place in terms of the film-maker's own culture.

In highly structured documentaries, the naturalisation process works on two levels. The first is the level of the technical/aesthetic where a film has not been made for profit only. **Rock Art Treasures,** for example, tries to establish a relationship between the figures painted by the !Kung on rocks with their wildlife environment. This is done by means of dissolves matching a stylised two-dimensional drawing of an animal with shots of real animals taken from the same angle. The visual result is to establish a romantic mystical relationship between the !Kung and their environment at the expense of anthropological explanation. Fragmentation for aesthetic and ideological effect is seen in **South Africa's Performing Arts.** The cultural heterogeneity of South Africa is compartmentalised into racial divisions which are made synonomous with musical styles. Whites are associated with classical music, and blacks with 'traditional' dancing.

The significance of events, interactions and relationships, however fundamental, may end up on the screen as trivia, with little connection to anything other than a 'beautiful' composition in the mind of the film-maker. The aesthetics of beauty, however, while cinematically functional to the film-maker, is discursive and purposive for the propagandists. 'Beauty' connects with the second level in the naturalisation process for it directs ideological closure to within the limits set by the ruling hegemony (whether political, anthropological or both).

In conventional documentaries the marriage of technique and ideology is geared to the interception of audience common sense (see, e.g., **The White Tribe of Africa** and **The South African Experience** where the codes are structured within a British liberal framework). Film-makers find themselves locked into a political economy which forces treatments of accepted themes to be in sympathy with the dominant system. It is not surprising, therefore, that television series like **The Tribal Identity** pander to entertainment oriented white audiences. The images Becker presented in this series under the discourse of anthropology legitimised the 'tribal' element of Nationalist apartheid ideology. Cameraman Lionel Friedberg's photography was entirely conventional for he always found the most beautiful way of shooting a particular scene, even to the extent of contradicting Becker's own reading of the situation.

Friedberg's later series, **They Came From the East,** however, did not revolve around clichés or the 'mysticism of the East'. Yet, as Van Zyl (1980b:23) points out, the series suffered from the problem of the 'special case': Indians who are socially, intellectually and financially indistinguishable from other South Africans were seen as 'different'. Van Zyl (1981) categorises **The Tribal Identity** as "institutionalised ethnography" which demonstrates all the problems associated with the demands made by a mass medium in the service of government. Of an even more crass nature are the films made by the Department of Information for crude propaganda purposes. A film like **Radio Bantu,** for example, is a slick well-made production which tries to hide its propagandist function behind 'creative' cinematic devices. While it does not try to strip away the accepted way of seeing things, the director is unable to prevent aberrant decoding for the camera techniques betray paternalism, state power and the class divisions of the South African social formation: whites are always seen in sharp dominant focus while blacks move 'rhythmically' in the background blur - they are always in silhouette, out of focus and muted. In **From the Assegai to the Javelin,** the very title suggest the 'civilising' influence of whites. This film starts off with the usual association of blacks with savagery. It implies that the substitution of the javelin, which has come from Western civilisation, for the assegaai, black warriors have been taught peaceful pursuits and to channel their innate aggression into sport and not war. Again, whites are dominant, in positions of authority, supervision and paternal control. A third example is **South Africa's Performing Arts** which associates 'arts' with 'buildings', and 'culture' with 'theatre-going', thus foreclosing any idea of 'performance' existing prior to the 19th Century, or within black society. Whites dominate, not only in terms of cultural imperialism, but also in terms of exposure in the film. This aesthetic view prevails, despite the narrator's claim that each culture influences the other.

The three examples given above serve to show that technique embodies ideological content and is legitimised through constant repetition in the majority of films that are seen. Through dramatization, the subject is 'brought alive' on the screen and therefore, "documentary determines the approach to a subject, but not necessarily the subject itself" (Rotha, 1936:133-4). There is a subtle distinction here between directors who are critically aware of the deep structures which underlie the economic contexts of what is being filmed, and those who merely take those contexts for granted. In the latter case, the means are primary, the purposes implicit to those means or techniques. In the former, the means, techniques and semiotic manipulations are conversely the door to representing images and relationships of actual conditions of existence. Ethnographic film differs from both of the above, in that its signifying procedures assume that the end cannot justify the means, for scientific results are only as reliable as the methodology which produces them.

OBSERVATIONAL CINEMA

Grierson and Rotha agreed that documentary's theoretical base was predicated upon the drawing of its material from a **sharing of experience** between the film-maker living within the subject community. The treatment and style of the film would emerge from this shared experience. Where the film-makers control the nature of that shared experience in the documentary form, in ethnographic film the process can be taken beyond observational cinema through reflexivity:

> By revealing his role, the film-maker enhances the value of his material as evidence. By entering actively into the world of his subjects, he can provoke a greater flow of information about them. By giving them access to the film, he makes possible the corrections, additions, and illuminations that only their response to the material can elicit. Through such an exchange a film can begin to reflect the ways in which its subjects perceive the world (MacDougall, 1975:119).

This was attempted to some extent by Holdstock with the subjects of **Indigenous Healers of Africa** and to a much greater degree by Hayman and Tomaselli with **I am Clifford Abrahams: This is Grahamstown.** The latter video was a co-production between a skilled television director, Hayman, and Abrahams, a coloured poverty-stricken alcoholic. Abrahams was drawn into the production process, shown how the technology worked and constantly consulted on-camera during the editing process. A video about how he 'makes out' through an ability to move through an extended network of social and racial spaces, the conventional relationship between the crew and the subject is collapsed as he becomes one

of the crew and the crew/cameras/tape recorder/microphone become part of the subject. Viewers are drawn into participation by
getting to know Abrahams from his perspective, one which is foregrounded over the interpretations of the crew.

It is rare that this democratic form of production finds its way into conventional documentary, particularly state sponsored films.
The power relationship is inexorably tilted in the direction of the
crew.

SOCIAL PROPAGANDA, POLITICAL PROPAGANDA

Because of documentary's connotative connections with propaganda, this form of film-making has been easily appropriated by the
dominant interests of society. Despite his political naïvety, Grierson was not unaware of how the documentary could become
debased and transformed into an ideological tool in the hands of
sectional interests (Tomaselli, 1984b). In the following extract he
discussed the subtle relationship between documentary and
propaganda in terms of his overall social objectives:

> The desire to make known and widely known the public ser-
> vices and social references they represent (government de-
> partments) was, in every sense, the opportunity for our docu-
> mentary art. Propaganda and art were at one in both mate-
> rial and policy. Documentary gave to propaganda an instru-
> ment it needed and propaganda gave to documentary a per-
> spective it needed. There was therefore virtue in the word
> 'propaganda', and even pride; and so it would continue for
> just as long as the service is really public and the reference
> really social. If, however, propaganda takes on its other more
> political meaning, the sooner documentary is done with the
> better (in Rotha, 1936:12).

The chapters that follow identify the greater part of South
African film dealing with people as propaganda with a political
meaning. They are therefore 'anthropologically useful' only in so
far as they tell the viewer something about the film-maker's culture and ideology. This argument also holds for the BBC productions about Afrikaners.

Since entertainment or propaganda is not the aim of ethnographic film, it is freer to discard cinematic conventions and cultural myths. Such films rely more on denotation than connotation. They try to cut through the myths that one society may have formed about another society. It is this shift in signification which differentiates **The Tribal Identity** from **They Came From the East.** Both of these series, however, continue to rely upon the codes and interpretants supplied by their viewers. This means that connotation and seeing individuals as 'special cases', for example, provide the ideological connections which allow such films to be easily interpreted from the point of view of the dominant apartheid ideology. Where conventions are severed and new techniques substituted, as was done with **On Becoming a Sangoma,** audience responses will differ depending on the interpreting structures supplied by the viewers. Those audiences which insist on experiencing 'the magic of Africa' will be disappointed for the field of significations presented will have little apparent relation to their mythical images. After its premiere at the Wits Ethnographic Film Festival in 1980, a number of viewers told me that this film was the most 'disgusting' they had ever seen. This response was governed by a process of overcoding which allowed them to bring prior conceptions to bear upon their interpretation of an undercoded text which was not unequivocal. In other words the significance of slaughtering the sacrificial animal and drinking its blood was not clearly spelt out. Viewers who objected to the apparent 'cruelty' and 'barbarism' of the ceremony, did so because they judged the slaughtering of animals outside its 'proper' context, that is in the confines of an abattoir, as 'gory' and 'uncivilised'. For these viewers, the film's portrayal of repeated motifs of animal slaughter outside its accepted 'civilised' context was incomprehensible and distressing.

Viewers who found **On Becoming a Sangoma** illuminating were able to make the semantic connections between the sacrifices and the appeasement of some higher deity, either through a parallel experience of other situations, or through being able to make connections in the implicit context in which the ceremonies took place. Since their interpreting structure had little sympathy for myths like 'magic' or romanticised portrayals of **sangomas,** the images they saw were not abduced as 'disgusting'. Their extracoding activity proceeded from the text as an empty form to which various possible meanings could be attributed. The codes selected by these viewers were those of anthropology and psychology and they thus accepted the film as a description of legitimate social behaviour.

DEFINITION OF ETHNOGRAPHIC FILM

Since this study is concerned with the analysis of already made films and television, it concentrates on films and videos 'about people' and 'about cultures'. The knowledge that informs the question of 'what to do with people' must be tied either to written anthropology or some other social science paradigm like holistic psychology. A theoretical perspective within which to order and connect observations, and by implication, the syntagma, is fundamental. Reflexivity and acknowledgement of the ethnographic presence, the ethnographic present and technology is an ethical and scientific responsibility. The definition should include the following symbiotic relationships:

(INTENTION)-Anthropologist-Producer-Process-Subjects-Audience-(PURPOSE)

The semiotics of ethnographic film, then, is the method by means of which we can study and account for the signs, codes and rules of inference that film-makers employ when making films/videos about people and cultures using a reflexive methodology and extracoding activity which produces metasemiotic statements in terms of an overtly stated anthropological/social science intention and purpose.

For the purposes of this study, we shall include films about people which are implicitly theoretical - even if only in terms of ideology - in order to discern non-reflexive films made with an ethnographic purpose from apparent ethnographic film with a political or propaganda purpose. Where intention is crucial to the above, effects are fundamental as far as non-reflexive films are concerned.

We are now in a position to measure the anthropologically usefulness of completed films and videos.

DEGREE OF ETHNOGRAPHICNESS

An application of the above criteria to the **criticism** of a film or video text will assist the researcher to measure the degree of ethnographicness of a production. This critical method is necessarily a **post hoc** process. The determination of this measurement is inversely proportional to the extent of intervention and manipulation of the film image and sound by the film-maker. Highly structured documentaries which deny their mediation exhibit a low quantity while a filmic ethnography meeting the conditions of our definition would show a high level. In either case, the baseline of measurement is the ethnographic understanding of the subjects rather than the ideological impositions of the producers.

EXTENT OF THE STUDY

The pages which follow do not attempt an exhaustive analysis of all the films which could be considered anthropologically useful, although detailed notes were taken of the majority of the 90 or so films listed in the filmography. The three chapters that follow have grouped the films according to themes. This chapter has offered the general outline within which the remainder may be considered.

CHAPTER 3

THEY CAME FROM THE EAST:
A STRUCTURED ABSENCES DISCOURSE

The purpose of this chapter is to apply some of the definitions and criteria of ethnographic film discussed in Chapter Two to specific examples of films and videos. It is an attempt to see how these productions approximate what might be termed, the 'ideal type' ethnographic film or alternatively, the extent to which they fall within the 'degrees of ethnographicness' outlined in the second chapter.

Inevitably the films dealt with here all fall into the 'anthropologically useful' category inasmuch as they satisfy what is perhaps the broadest definition of ethnographic film, that of films being "about people" (Heider, 1972). The method of criticism applied is necessarily a post hoc process because there appears to be no apparent intention on behalf of the producers to adhere to basic ethnographic production principles. This is certainly the case with Lionel Friedberg's **They Came from the East** which adheres more to classic documentary style than to the principles of ethnographic film.

In this chapter we look specifically at Friedberg's **They Came from the East.** The major focus will be on the degree to which it subscribes to the notion of a 'filmic ethnography'. More specifically, the analysis incorporates the discourse of structured absences (Gavshon, 1980; Tomaselli, 1983b). For the purposes of definition these two areas will be dealt with as separate entities but in the final applied analysis they will be fused in a general critique of the series.

The degree to which any film is judged ethnographic necessarily requires that it incorporates certain of the basic elements discussed in Chapter Two. They include holism, ethnographic presence, and the ethnographic present. For our purposes it is more important to see to what extent Friedberg's intuitive approach approximates the ethnographic principles discussed in Chapter Two.

Friedberg has indicated that he had no intention of producing an ethnographic document although an attempt at intercultural communication was one of his "driving motives" (Interview, 19 April 1984). Clearly then it was not his intention to produce anything other than a documentary which only incidentally falls within the realm of ethnographic film. However, this by no means detracts from seeing the series as manifesting ethnographic potential. The mere fact that there is an apparent absence of ethnographic intention does not immediately disqualify the series from the realm of ethnography.

THE CAME FROM THE EAST: A CRITIQUE

The series was commissioned by SABC-TV in 1976. While Friedberg acknowledges that few guidelines were given, or constraints imposed on the making of the series, it appears it was to be categorised as an exercise in 'intercultural communication'. Friedberg's brief was to "make three programmes (later increased to six) looking at the Indian South Africans" (Interview, 19 April 1984). He was chosen to produce the series because of previous dealings with the SABC, especially as producer of the **Tribal Identity** series which was screened during the SABC's first year of transmission. Previous productions also included a forerunner to **Tribal Identity** entitled **Cultural Identity,** which was made for the Department of Foreign Affairs for overseas consumption. The latter film can be characterised as propaganda in support of 'separate development'. The film was part of a rationalisation of apartheid according to the need for each cultural group within the 'mosaic of South African cultures' to recognise and assert a distinctive and organic culture. Clearly then, Friedberg had previously produced material which the state found palatable and which neither questioned nor challenged the dominant ideology. This is not to suggest that Friedberg was a willing propagandist or that he was even aware of the uses to which his films were to be put. It is likely he saw his role merely as a neutral film-maker with the specific intention of producing a series which matched up to his own high standards of production excellence.

They came from the East is a six-part series dealing with the history, culture and politics of South Africans who originally emigrated here from India. It involves a chronological sequence from the arrival, problems and hardships encountered by the first indentured labourers in 1868. The series ends with a cursory analysis of contemporary South African Indian political and social aspirations. The balance of the programmes deal with such elements of culture as dance, religion, ritual and education. Sources for the series include extensive use of a selected number of interviewees, books, illustrative actuality shot on location in Durban, and relevant historical sites. These sources are expertly woven together with the appropriate narration and music to produce an informative documentary. As argued in Chapter Two, it is an error to see this, or any documentary as ideologically neutral. It is not the intention of this chapter to be overly critical of the content of the series, though the depictions of history were found to be accurate (Kuper, 1960; Huttenback, 1976; Tomaselli, R. 1983). Such a critique would not necessarily assist in an understanding of the programmes as an ethnographic/ideological document. Instead we will adopt what Gavshon (1980), Tomaselli (1983b) and Heck (1980) have termed 'structured absences'.

Structured Absences

According to Gavshon (1980) structured absences is a critical concept with which to look at the 'decentered' relationship between the text and its context. This method uncovers what is absent in relation to what is present:

> What will be attempted here through a prescansion of these films is a process of active reading, is to make them say what they have to say within what they leave unsaid, to reveal their constituent lacks; these are neither faults in the work ... nor a deception on the part of the author ... they are structuring absences, always displaced ... the unsaid included in the said and necessary to its constitution. In short to use Althusser's expression - the 'internal shadows of exclusion' (**Cahiers du Cinema**, 1970:6).

Gavshon goes on to say that the method seeks to find "certain points of tension or 'structuring absences'" (Gavshon, 1980:47).

Put more simply, instead of considering what the film says by identifying the structured absences, we can expose the hidden ideological discourse by looking at what is not said on the paradigmatic selection axis.

Heck (1980) supports the view that both structured absences or what he calls the "non-manifest organisation of the message" as well as the manifest content of the message need to be considered: "When a message is emitted it is not only what is 'said' that has significance but also the 'way' it is said" (Heck, 1980: 24). Here Heck acknowledges that what is included and excluded from the text is of importance. He further indicates that what is said needs to be analysed closely according to the way the message is organised. As we shall show, the codes used in Friedberg's production were designed to prevent aberrant decoding with respect to white audiences. Indian viewers, however, used a different interpretative code which led them to be more critical of the series. Heck believes that an analysis of the latent organisation of the message through either inclusion or exclusion of content is necessary to define ideology. He sees ideology as "a system of semantic rules which express a certain level of organisation of messages". It is through the disentangling of these semantic rules that we can get to the core of a message, where the "core" includes both manifest and non-manifest organisation. In summary then, Heck believes that the selection and combination of messages is reflexive of the ideological point of view of the general social, political or economic context in which the film is made. More specifically it is reflexive of the ideological position of the producer.

This present critique, however, is not solely concerned with absences but also with the ideological tensions manifested by what is considered. For example, Friedberg uses the South African Indian Council (SAIC) as his political reference point throughout the series. At no time does he consider the political views or activities of the vibrant anti-SAIC organisations operating at the time the series was made. They include a multiplicity of community-based organisations. The text is thus an ideological statement resulting from what is considered (the exclusive use of established political forums such as SAIC and the reformist politics that characterises it). An ideological statement also arises from what is not considered (mass based opposition to SAIC elections at the time the series was being produced). In both cases there are 'decentered relationships between the text and its context'. In the former case we see SAIC (manifested in the text) as being solely representative of Indian political opinion because of the absence of alternative political organisations (the context). In the latter case we see a similar decentred text/context relationship where the text (the visual or verbal content of the series) excludes alternative opinion. The context, or the sum total of what actually occurred as mediated through newspaper coverage, subsequent political analyses and through individual experience, indicates a very different situation from what is contained in the series.

It is important to stress that the ideological distortions resulting from what is considered and what is not considered do not necessarily reflect "a fault ... (or) a deception on the part of the author" (Gavshon, 1980:47). It is very likely that the director was not aware of contemporary alternative political views. Alternatively, if aware of them, his selection of content and sources were governed by a sophisticated understanding (or gut reaction) of what would have been acceptable to the SABC and/or its target audience. The inclusion of oppositional perspectives would have jeopardised the sale of the series and, as a result, the transmission.

The Ethnographic Presence

Friedberg introduces **They Came from the East** with a sequence of himself sitting on an editing table and addressing the camera directly. Amongst other things he states:

> The history of South Africa is based on a wide range of sources ... and people are drawn from a wide mosaic of cultures and backgrounds. One such place is India ... it became clear that it would be impossible to incorporate everything into a single generalised account of the Indian social scene and lifestyle. We have tried to capture the essence of things but it's really the Indian people themselves who will be telling their own story (Episode 1).

This introduction requires an in-depth analysis both for the method he used to set the foundations and parameters of the series, and for its actual content. On the face of it, it appears that Friedberg, intentionally or unintentionally, has adopted one of the most important criteria of ethnographic film production - reflexivity through the presence of the director on the film itself. This form of reflexivity is rare in most of the films considered for this study. The majority of South African made ethnographic films have attempted to submerge the presence of camera and crew, either through ignorance of accepted ethnographic production techniques, or because their stated intention was to produce a documentary which purposefully excludes ethnographic presence. As argued in Chapter Two, documentary film exhibits a lack of methodology and a conspicuous absence of scientific justifications for the decisions made by the crew during the production process (Ruby, 1977).

Friedberg does create a presence but it cannot be seen as an ethnographic presence in the strict sense of the definition. Firstly, his visual presence is limited to the opening (Episode 1) and closing (Episode 6) of the series. For the intervening four episodes he maintains a narrators presence. However, a narrators presence is very different from a physical presence. The narrator in direct address comes across as the Voice of Authority, rather than of the personal impressions of the observer.

Friedberg's opening and closing sequences then do not constitute ethnographic presence. His limited reflexivity does not situate him as film-maker within the context of the movie. Neither does it make any significant contribution to the audiences' understanding of the extent to which the film crew has distorted or reinterpreted the subjects' behaviour.

A close analysis of the content of the reflexive addresses indicates an attempt to define definite parameters or limits within which Friedberg intended operating. They are pointers to what Friedberg himself admitted was a "personal voyage ... à la Alister Cooke style". Furthermore, both the introduction and conclusion serve to implicitly absolve Friedberg of any responsibility for what is about to, or has, appeared. There is a sense of him setting himself up as neutral 'bridge' between Indian subjects and predominantly white viewers. His programmes are the vehicles through which information between subject group and recipient is communicated. Friedberg's opening and closing sequences, then, do not constitute the ethnographic presence in the strict sense. Rather, his presence is a limited, but deflected reflexivity. It acknowledges the Producer, but only brief aspects of Process - that interpretations will be offered from a white perspective. The lack of a sustained presence limits the audiences' understanding of the extent to which the film crew distorted or reinterpreted their subjects' behaviour.

From the above we can identify a contradiction between Fried-berg's stated intention for the series to be a "personal voyage", while at the same time stressing the pursuit of objectivity by having the Indians 'tell their own story'. This common sense is by no means incidental or unusual but reflects a traditional mis-apprehension on the part of documentary film-makers about their perceived neutrality in the production process. It also relates to the generally ill-defined nature of the documentary form where a coherent methodology or need for scientific justification is not always considered necessary by producers. Under the circum-stances, it is little wonder documentary has been so successfully adopted by propagandist and social reformer alike.

Separatist Discourse

Throughout the series Friedberg makes repeated references to a "mosaic of cultures and backgrounds". The notion of a conglome-ration of separate cultures is a recurring concept in apartheid dis-course (as well as many of the films viewed for this study) and implicitly suggests a separation of the races. Furthermore, one gets the impression of a culturally coherent 'community' that is isolated from, and unaffected by the balance of South Africa's people. This use of "accepted labels" in the programme consis-tently obscures the strife and divisions within the 'community'. Friedberg acknowledged that his use of the term 'community' was governed by the official separatist discourse:

> Yes, well one is secularising people certainly, but we did make the film in South Africa. It was for the SABC and in the South African context there are separate communities. They are known as such and they are labelled as such. One

has to prepare it that way. If one had to talk about the 'Indian people' without going to the community level, you would find an adverse reaction from the Indians themselves. The Muslims and the Hindus do regard each other as separate communities although they might be labelled under the Department of Indian Affairs and therefore they are a singular community. But amongst themselves they do not regard themselves that way ... They are separate. In fact the Tamil Hindus regard themselves as being very separate from reformed Hindus. We did make this film for a white audience and they regard them as being the 'Indians' and so, if one is going to talk about separate aspects of 'the Indians', you are going to talk about that aspect of the community. It's very difficult and it's very delicate. How does one invent labels which go beyond the accepted labels? (Interview, 19.4.84).

While it may be argued that the subject group needed to be clearly identified and delineated for the purpose of treating them filmicly, the narration nevertheless supports separatist ideology in the absence of adhering to the proper meaning of 'community' as a group of people living in the same area and having common interests (MacIver, 1931; Smelser, 1967; Phillips, 1969; Tomaselli, 1984a). By taking the state's meaning of 'community' for granted, the director is unable to prevent the process of overcoding where an interpretation is imposed on a group of people who have little more in common than that of ancestry and skin hue. This skewed emphasis is the result of the need to prepare the text to intercept the common sense codes of a white audience. The director's intention thus vitiated the ethnographic integrity of the film in terms of the perspectives that he knew would be appropriate in terms of budgetary, institutional and ideological constraints. Because the means of mental production is controlled by the SABC and its sub-contractors, the propensity toward overcoding activity on the part of the white viewer is enhanced. This was apparently borne out by the positive comment by whites, as opposed to a largely negative response by Indian audiences. Ultimately, this displacement of meaning is the result of an inequable power relationship which facilitates the construction of a skewed code which has seemingly ethnographic qualities. The inequable power relationship between the film-makers and their subjects is further indicated by the almost total absence of whites in the series.

Consideration of those whites who are included and the way they are portrayed reflects the ideological position of society from which the producer emanates. In **They Came from the East,** whites are almost always portrayed in positions of authority, or as anomalies in an exclusively Indian world. We see whites as heads of Indian educational institutions, namely of Sultan College and the University of Durban-Westville. The two educationists were included because of "their positions". Later, we see a close-up of a white man, woman and child participating in a ceremony at the Rama Krishna Centre. Significantly there are no other whites in the congregation and the camera makes a play on this obvious social and religious anomaly. Although the presence of the couple and child are extraordinary in the context of the all-Indian series and unusual in the context of a Hindu ceremony, there is nevertheless a sense that the camera highlights their presence in order to project a false cosmopolitancy and social intercourse which contradicts the usual South African perception of reality. Friedberg also explains the absence of whites on purely pragmatic grounds saying that it was his intention to introduce the Indians to the whites in South Africa:

> and so, of course we concentrated on the Indians. That was the whole motive behind the making of the programme. We didn't purposefully exclude whites but we were talking to the Indians and listening to what they were all about (Interview, 19.4.84).

One recalls John van Zyl's (1980b) point about Indians being categorised as "special cases". What informs this pigeonholing is dependent upon the methodologies used. A class analysis, for example, would have identified the similarities rather than the differences. It would appear therefore that the series has the effect of communicating existing dominant/dominated class relations while at the same time trying to break down these existing class relations through the inclusion of symbolic whites as anomalies.

While Friedberg is careful not to portray a 'utopian' Indian world inasmuch as he deals with genuine social, political and economic concerns, he nevertheless portrays an exclusively Indian world where real class relations are significantly absent. We do see and hear occasional references to differing social groups based on language or caste, but these hardly suggest intragroup class relations. The more significant absence of class relations must be seen in terms of the absence of whites as hegemonic, as well as the myth that Indians are able to exist as an organic, autonomous group within the South African social formation.

In terms of the structured absences discourse there are other areas which require consideration. There is a significant lack of interviewees who may be termed 'non-achievers' in the conventional sense of the word. Most interviewees were carefully selected by virtue of their prominence in their chosen fields. We are presented with heads of educational institutions, successful entrepreneurs, political leaders and so on. There is an almost total absence of the working class who constitute the majority of South African Indians. When we do see them, they are portrayed in the working context (i.e. factories) and are used merely as background material. None of them are given the opportunity to voice alternative viewpoints. Friedberg explained this absence in terms of both institutional and cultural constraints:

> Again it is perhaps a time factor. Within the boundaries of six programmes, covering a subject as broad as this, you really can't have as many interviews as you would like to have. Talking heads do not make good TV - but I'm not trying to skirt the issue and I'm not trying to get out of it that way. I had to be very careful about this. The Muslim woman, although very closeted, is very much more a professional person than the Hindu. The Hindu woman is the one behind the sewing machine and the one kneading the bread in the bakery, whereas the Muslim woman who goes out to work is invariably the one who becomes the lawyer. You have to be very careful about how you portray all of this. Perhaps now one would be able to do this more openly, but at the time it was an introduction to what the Indian people are and how the women have defined their own role within their own community and in the broader community of South Africa. It's not an excuse for not going into greater detail but what was possible at the time (Interview, 19.4.84).

In cases where contentious topics are dealt with, the treatment is often inadequate, and tends to favour an official point of view.

For instance, housing is glossed over. A brief sequence of shanty houses is rapidly followed by shots of opulent housing. The juxta-position of the interviewees is contradictory, saying 'yes, there's that, but on the other hand there's this'. Again, Friedberg cites institutional limitations to account for an under-emphasis on the housing shortage:

> Of course we did make this for the SABC and that kind of thing was semi-taboo at the time and you really couldn't delve too much into the housing shortage. The fact that we did mention it and that it did get on TV (for the first time) was a breakthrough. Today in **News Focus** they might take the situation further. But this was 1978 and we couldn't talk too much about that (Interview, 19.4.84).

Under the circumstances it is difficult to imagine that a documentary concerned with "what the Indian people have to say about themselves" could exclude the views or at least a filmic consideration of the majority of the South African Indians. An acknowledgement of those constraints on the video is the only path open to the film-makers who are forced to deny access to alternative viewpoints. However, in the context of the SABC - "even this may be impossible."

Political Reassurance

The process of building up and breaking down is a consistent technique running throughout the series and is repeated at various levels. On occasion, individuals are openly critical of political and educational issues including the Group Areas Act and restraints, particularly of business opportunities. Inevitably though, the interviewees qualify their criticism with a seemingly unfounded confidence in the status quo. In a closing sequence (Episode 6) we see a doctor who had previously spelt out his dissatisfaction with the existing order in no uncertain terms, reassuring his son that reform would be forthcoming and that to establish roots in South Africa would not be in vain.

Sources
Throughout the series there is the continual use of a limited num-

ber of interviewees. As already indicated they are all, without exception, 'achievers' in their particular chosen fields. The continuous use of the same interviewees reflects both time and financial constraints. A more disturbing criteria for selection was the interviewees' command of English and the extent to which they were able to articulate sometimes complex and abstract phenomena. This is particularly true of the female academic and dance teacher at the University of Durban-Westville who explains the intricacies of traditional dance. According to Friedberg the reason for using her was because she was a

> very respected member of the community ... The Indian background is amazing and I thought that she (explained it very well) and her English was very good (Interview, 19.4.84).

In one broad stroke, Friedberg has included a plethora of social, political, religious and cultural issues which, of necessity, he has had to deal with on an extremely superficial level. There are exceptions. These include the programmes on religion and dance. In these two specific cases it appears that detailed treatment resulted from easily available source material and the non-contentious nature of the activity, rather than as a result of their supposed importance in the lives of the average South African Indian. When asked what criteria he used to include or exclude aspects of education, culture and religion in his original script, Friedberg admitted that the importance of the series lay not so much in what was said, but rather, in what was left out:

> One had to perhaps, not Westernise it, but bring it all down to make it understandable ... logical ... acceptable ... credible to a Western-type audience. What one had to do was to extract what was the best, the most pertinent and the most acceptable bits and pieces. We then had to make it work in a way people would understand (Interview, 19.4.84).

Clearly Friedberg was guided not so much by rules of social scientific procedure but by a personal sense of what was relevant to a white audience. Any possibility of ideological distortion as a result of this personal selection is countered by his insistence that he was guided by "some very good people". Paradigmatic selection of available sources is always a problem and even though his choices fell on those working within the legitimate consensus,

Friedberg still "got a lot of flack from a lot of Indians" because he constructed his codes within the field of significations which naturalised the hegemonic myths of the white target audience.

Concept of Truth

A more disturbing guideline that Friedberg appears to have adopted is an overriding desire for the 'truth'. In a somewhat tortuous statement he says,

> I wanted to tell the truth and I wanted to present it in as balanced a way as possible bearing in mind that the programmes were being made for white viewers who, on average, knew very, very little about the Indians.

The implication of this statement is that the presentation of 'truth' is possible and then ties the attainment of that truth to the need to satisfy a white audience.

If, as was argued in Chapter Two, the 'reality' or truth of any situation is tied to technological and subjective constraints, then we need to look at how these criteria affected **They Came from the East.** It is already evident that a scientific methodology is conspicuously absent in the series. Friedberg worked from a limited number of "guiding sources" amongst which was an Indian member of the SABC Advisory Board who supplied him with "some idea on paper as to what should be mentioned and depicted". Friedberg goes on to state that apart from the Indian community themselves there are little or no other sources. While in Durban for a three week fact-finding mission he "probed and dug and turned up a lot of stones and knocked on many doors and met as many people as I could." It was these people who provided the framework and parameters around which the final production was structured. He also states that an overriding concern was an attempt at facilitating 'intercultural communication'. Once again a definition of this somewhat misused concept is not given, especially the extent to which it governed selection and organisation of raw material. Like the much abused term 'community', the idea of 'intercultural communication' also derives its meaning from its ideological usages rather than its proper TWO-WAY **raison d'être.** It would appear that the common sense discourse of this form of communication is seen by the state as a means of selling the 'benefits' of apartheid. Resistance is only seen to occur in cases where this 'communication' has broken down. Rectification of this 'communication lapse' is offered as the solution to the restoration of stability (see Fourie, 1981; Tomaselli, 1983b).

Technological and other objective constraints on production included a surprisingly small production crew and limited time and money. In total there were three members of the production crew. They included Friedberg as cameraman alternating as sole interviewer, an assistant cameraman and a sound man. Friedberg directed all questions from behind and to one side of the camera and all questions were later edited out. The net result is a slick, fast moving documentary which rarely subscribes to the attributes of reflexivity through ethnographic presence. When questioned why he felt it necessary to exclude all evidence of the production crew or camera, Friedberg said it was "just basic good film-making". This response recalls Ruby's (1977) criticism of the uncritical acceptance of the documentary form as the only necessary explanatory parameters.

Clearly, a rigorous scientific methodology for selection of material and the final edit are totally absent. It appears that decisions were governed by both objective considerations of money, time and availability of willing sources as well as subjective notions of what Friedberg personally perceived to constitute the discourse of "good film-making".

CONCLUSION

Friedberg described his series as a "voyage" which is "not a definitive ethnographic exercise ... or a document on the Indian community", but one in which "The Indians had their own say":

They made their comments, be they adverse, negative, positive, whatever, and I merely served as a bridge to link those
things together in terms of being the Voyager through those
people, through their problems, through their lifestyles,
through their whatever.

His discussion on the series nevertheless highlights most of the
theoretical points dealt with in Chapter Two. Friedberg's intuitive reaction that **They Came from the East** is not ethnography,
exhibits a rare and refreshing acknowledgement of the limits of
documentary, and of the problems facing the white director trying
to encode "what THEY wanted US to say about the community"
for the "white viewer, not the Indians".

Friedberg was also keenly aware of the problems of structured absences: "In any documentary, in the final analysis, when you look
back on it in retrospect, the programmes don't really consist of
what you said but of what you really have to leave out". He
qualified this observation saying, "And for me that was the most
painful aspect of it". The producer clearly had an acute
understanding of the institutional constraints and consensual
discourse he would have to negotiate in the production of the
series. Apart from his objective of wanting "the white South
African to meet his Indian counterpart", further intentions were to
'break new ground' politically in terms of airing Indian objections
to the Group Areas Act and dissatisfaction with state housing
policy (Episode 6). Again, it is rare that film-makers are able to
conceptualise their practice in theoretical terms, even if only
intuitively. This understanding of how texts signify, together with
a knowledge of institutional gate-keeping mechanisms, provided
him the opportunity to extend the boundaries of the SABC
consensual discourse. However, as was argued in Chapter Two,
the struggle for meaning is a two-way process. That the SABC
accepted the series without modification is indicative of shifting
political attitudes which were to culminate in the President's
Council in 1984. The effect of the series, broadcast in 1980, was
to introduce white South Africans to South African Indians in such
a way that this new political dispensation would be legitimised and
accepted by whites.

We may recall our definition of ethnographic film enunciated in
the first chapter:

(INTENT)-Anthropologist-Producer-Process-Subjects-Audience-PUR-POSE)

Friedberg's intention may not have been the same as that of the SABC. So too will PURPOSE differ. That of the film-maker's was clearly ethnographic. Friedberg, though claiming that the series is "not ethnography", consistently talks about it in terms reminiscent of Heider (1972). The series thus tells us as much about the ideo-logy and culture of the film-makers, as it does about the subjects. The Anthropologist is missing in the equation but there was a sys-tematic reliance upon written (e.g. Kuper, 1960) as well as archi-val and 'expert' sources. The Producer identifies himself in two of the six programmes. It is Process and Subjects, however, which are the weak points of the equation. Because Friedberg relies un-questioningly on the codes of 'good film-making', he does not encode his methodology, though he is aware of its strengths and weaknesses as is evidenced in his interview with the authors. Allied to this is a rather muddled conception of 'truth', that the 'truth' would come through a 'balanced' treatment and the codes of good film-making. In Chapter Two, we discussed in some detail the problems of the idea of an objective truth out-there waiting to be captured by merely using cinematic codes.

Although a number of Indians were consulted at the editing stage, it is doubtful that any suggestions that conflicted with form would have been acted upon. Friedberg estimated a 30% negative res-ponse from his subjects. The target audience of white South Af-ricans (69,4% of all viewers) was generally positive. As Friedberg notes of the differing reactions: "The double-sided response that I got showed the chasm that really existed between the whites and the Indians. We bridged a little bit of it". The "chasm", however, is really more one of Producer-interpretation for such a series should ideally have the acceptance of the subjects as well as the intended white audience. The apparent reason for the 30% Indian dissension was precisely because of the desire to represent all In-dians in South-Africa as members of one 'community', an inte-grated group of people with a coherent culture in terms of "accepted labels". It was this assumption of separatist discourse that must have resulted in the largely negative Indian reaction (who made up 7% of the viewing audience). The director was quite aware of the dissensions between groups of people who had originally emigrated to South Africa from India. Furthermore, much of his research indicated that South African 'Indians' are not a group or a community in the proper sense of these terms:

> The Indian community is a very complex community with lots of diverse viewpoints and different aspirations. The community itself is pigeonholed into lots of different areas. I was particularly surprised at the amount of conflict I found amongst the Indians - particularly on the South African situation. But I extracted as much as I could from all of those and then asked: how does one boil all this down, including bits of all of it, if this is what they are all about, if this is what they believe in. How much of this do I really represent? I really tried to mix it all together and present as much as possible from all points of view.

However, these conflicts were absent from the series. They were absent because they identified points of tension about white hegemony and because they indicated that, contrary to the accepted political common sense, the Indian 'community' is not a community. Rather, that group of people who originally came from India is a disparate collection of groups, class fractions and perhaps specific territorially-bound communities, sometimes allied and sometimes divided between themselves, all of whom are repressed on ethnic grounds.

The final component of the equation is PURPOSE. This is the crucial element in defining its degree of ethnographicness. We have seen that the series was governed by the institutional and political discourse of the state. Its acceptance by the SABC - a body well known to serve the direct interests of the National Party (Wilkins and Strydom, 1978; Crankshaw et al, 1983; Hayman, 1986) - suggests that the series was produced within the specific historical conjuncture which allowed a degree of criticism of the state as it tested the ground for a new political 'dispensation' designed to include the 'Indian population group' on unequal terms in the central government. In this context of transmission, the series must exhibit a low degree of ethnographicness as the purpose of screening is political and the audience, both white and Indian, would perceive it as such.

Seen in a different context, the series would exhibit a greater ethnographic integrity, and is a measure of both white perceptions and some 'Indian' cultural responses to life in South Africa. The final, very important point that needs to be made concerns the typing of people into 'communities' in terms of their skin colour. This is in itself an ideologically motivated ethnographic category which in the South African case, has the effect of legitimising the separatist discourse of apartheid.

The domain of the anthropologist, therefore, lies not only with the description of other cultures, but with an examination of the ideological underpinnings of the scientific discourse which is very often deployed to 'prove' political positions.

CHAPTER 4

INTERNATIONAL AND
LOCAL MYTHS ABOUT AFRIKANERS

The present chapter is less concerned with ethnography per se than the previous chapters. It deals with television series and films which purport to examine ethnographic criteria, but under the guise of documentary. It will be recalled that we defined documentary as a code which organises messages in a particular way. The form of this style of film-making governs the parameters of method in an invisible discourse. We shall therefore attempt to discuss the BBC-TV series, **The White Tribe of Africa** in terms of the hidden messages encoded by foreign producers in films about the Afrikaner. This will be followed by analysis of films made by the South African state which try to counter the arguments presented in foreign television series.

A number of films which investigate the Afrikaner objective of separate development have appeared since 1960. Each of these - **South Africa Loves Jesus, The Defiant White Tribe, The White Laager, The White Tribe of Africa** - try to explain apartheid in terms of the arguments presented by the Afrikaner, but against the background of British liberal ideology. We will concentrate only on **The White Tribe of Africa**. Readers wishing to follow up some of the other series are referred to Hall (1976), **FLQ** (1976), **Cineaste** (1976), Tomaselli (1981b) and Safford (1981).

The messages of most of the above films are occasioned by the South African practice of racial capitalism (Saul and Gelb, 1981) or apartheid which is interpreted as a purely Afrikaner cultural phenomenon. Although South Africa is of military and economic importance to the West, its spatial organisation of society is, paradoxically, portrayed as having little connection with Western capitalism. National cultures founded on capitalism present themselves as exemplars of such ideals as 'freedom' and 'equality'. They feel it incumbant upon themselves to castigate a group who they fear might bring into disrepute the political economy on which Western culture is founded. The 'solution' to this political impasse is to present a picture of South African history and political economy as the result of the machinations of a deviant 'ethnic' group - as shown by such titles as **The Defiant White Tribe, The White Tribe of Africa** and **The White Laager.**

The ideology of the Afrikaner group is abstracted from its political and economic foundations and is presented as a pre-industrial hang-up, a fanatical adherence to cultural and historical symbols and a fight for Afrikaner survival against all odds. The interpretation of the South African situation denies a class analysis of the state and thus presumes that Afrikaners are a homogeneous group without internal fragmentation such as the verligte or verkrampte tendencies. This ahistorical account ignores the role played by British imperialism in the proletarianisation of the Afrikaner. It is unaware of the subsequent development of Afrikaner nationalism as a response to the penetration of British capital into the South African economy. Absent from these series are depictions of English-speaking South Africans and the supportive role they have played in maintaining the role of capital within racial capitalism. It is against this background that we will analyse the four-part series, **The White Tribe of Africa.**

IDEOLOGICAL GAZE AND THE 'WHITE TRIBE OF AFRICA'

Three types of 'gaze' can be identified in film analysis: (1) the camera's original gaze; (2) the viewer made to identify with the gaze of the proponent of the dominant textual ideology; and (3) the gaze within the film (Kaplan, 1978). This schema is useful in examining the structure and levels of signification in **The White Tribe of Africa.** The camera's gaze can be best understood as the overall socio-political and economic context which motivates the making of the film. In this case, the operation of the BBC-TV production crew (which included a number of South Africans) took place within the consensus of the liberal capitalist discourse prevalent in Britain. Hence, the camera's gaze in **The White Tribe of Africa** is a cinematic reflection and confirmation of liberal ideology.

The film-maker directs the viewer's gaze so that she/he identifies with this British liberal ideology. In **The White Tribe of Africa,** the interviewer, David Dimbleby, is both 'film-maker' and 'actor'.

As actor he becomes a signifier: he signifies the ideology of liberal capitalism which he espouses in the act of making the series. Thus the viewer's gaze is directed by Dimbleby, and often at Dimbleby, so that the former identifies with the ideology that he signifies.

As signifier Dimbleby manipulates the viewer's gaze to suit a given interpretation within the ideology he represents. Thus despite the fact that the camera's gaze is within a capitalist framework, that is, capitalist Britain gazing at capitalist South Africa, we can distinguish different orientations within this framework. Thus Dimbleby, as signifier, ensures that the viewer's gaze sometimes sympathises with the Afrikaners when they identify a poor struggling people trying to find a new Jerusalem. At other times the viewers are made to see the Afrikaner as a heartless monster. Afrikanerdom and apartheid are constituted as the object of the viewer's gaze as though they were from an experience radically different from British imperialism and capitalism. They are not: by objectifying them in this way, capital can stand aloof, insinuate a difference, and hence castigate an 'other' (in the Sartrean sense) so as to absolve itself of the practices it is castigating.

The gaze within the series directs us to the textual conflicts: Afrikaner against 'black' South African; and Afrikaner against 'Briton' - both historically, and in the making of the programmes. This gaze is exemplified by PW Botha's steady, supercilious gaze at the interviewer (who signifies British liberal capitalism and for an Afrikaner, British imperialism). The camera zooms in to close-up and very close-up shots which capture Botha's steely eyes and the disparagement in his gaze. The action of the camera engages our sympathy for the interviewer (both as signifier and signified), and thus confirms the presentation of Botha as a symbol of apartheid ideology, denying its links with responsible capitalism.

The object of the various gazes in the series is myth. There are myths on both sides of the camera: the myth of the 'oppositional' film-maker seeking truth and challenging a chimera; and the myth of the white tribe of Africa. We shall examine the myth of the film-director first.

The Director and Objectivity

Roland Barthes (1973) has described a myth as a chain of related concepts which form the connotation of the signified. When the letters 'BBC' flash onto the screen, they become a signifier for the structure of the BBC, and the second order meaning of this signified is the myth of the BBC: that is, that the station produces programmes which are 'impartial' 'balanced' and 'objective'. Yet these very qualities are used to locate the programmes within the consensus of the dominant liberal ideology which informs the practice of television production in the United Kingdom. This structure of production confirms the myth of the liberal-humanism of the British, who could be seen as a metonym for the West. This is clear from a sequence regarding the West which is used in the text of the series. The interviewer asks Botha what he feels about the West's attitude to South Africa's apartheid policies. Here the interviewer and 'the West' signify 'proponents of humanism and freedom', and Botha and South Africa signify oppression. Thus the interviewer locates himself within the ideology of the freedom-loving Western capitalist democracies, and his product, the films, are seen both as a confirmation of his position, and as a means of penetrating an opposing situation.

The text has a complex structure because there is a constant interplay between the two myths. The interviewer is at the nexus of this interplay: he is not an independent information gathering source, but a signifier. He signifies the liberal democratic side of the 'balance' paradigm, which is placed in opposition to the undemocratic forces signified by the Afrikaner, the 'white' tribe of Africa.

The Myths of the 'White' Tribe

Dimbleby presents the myth of the Afrikaner by creating two images of them: (1) of a beleaguered group of people trying to seek a place of freedom and peace in an alien and hostile milieu; and (2) an inscrutable enigma ruling South Africa. The first myth is predicated upon images of rural settler folk; their cherished ideal of finding a new land; their innocence and naivety, but also tenacity and courage in the face of hardships; their strong religious convictions; their triumph, seen as a gift from God and a justification for their actions. This myth comes straight from the paradigm of colonialism presented by colonisers.

The liberal film-maker, however, also presents 'the other side'. The Afrikaner also signifies a monstrous machinery of oppression indicated by the police and armed forces. The very machine-like bureaucracy is also portrayed as being an inaccessible enigma. This myth of 'oppressor' is propounded in various ways in the series. For instance, a 'black' woman student who is interviewed describes the Afrikaners as "stupid". We see an image of her putting her finger to her head, a sign which indicates the irrationality of the group about whom she is talking. A second example concerns a 'white' man and 'coloured' woman who cannot marry because they have been classified differently. They both speak of Afrikaners as if they were a breed apart. They suggest that things might have been different if the government had been of English stock. The couple simply do not "understand" the Afrikaner mind.

By emphasising the tribal aspect of the Afrikaners as portrayed in the myth, the film-maker removes them from a paradigm which could explain them and their policies in terms of the capitalist ideology on which the South African and British economies are predicated. We need to ask two questions: Firstly, is the government policy inscrutable and irrational, and secondly, if it is not, then why does the director present it this way? One could suggest that South African policy is perfectly clear, ascertainable, and rational in terms of its ideology of racial capitalism. A possible reason why the series presents the National Party policies as inscrutable and irrational is that they operate from within the same ideological field as British libertarianism. The only objections 'fair-minded' Britons have is to the institutionalisation of racism (which might hinder the workings of international monopoly capitalism). Apartheid is therefore presented as being economically irrational because the film-maker - through his ahistorical analysis - is unable to identify the class basis of how this contributes to a brutal form of capitalism.

Verbal Codes

The verbal code is pre-eminent in establishing the director's view of the South African situation. This is effected by the kind of questions he poses. These are informed by a humanist ideology, which borders on sentiment, for example, "How do you feel about ...". These questions are put to both 'black' and 'white' persons, and each answer is articulated in terms of personal feelings. Thus a situation arises in which we have PW Botha (ex-Minister of Defence) saying that he "regrets every death in detention" as he is of a "Christian" people. A viewer who aberrantly decodes this from a different ideological perspective would see the irony in this statement, but there is no sign in the diegetic sequence which suggests this. As a result of this method of enquiry, the structures underlying the situations investigated are never the object of the discussions. In contrast, Anthony Thomas' **Six Days in Soweto** hammers home its irony in a crude manner that simply could not be misunderstood by any audience (Tomaselli, 1981b).

The interviewer maintains a semblance of 'balance' by interviewing 'all' sides:

1. Afrikaner 'whites' in authority, for example, Brigadier Visser of the Soweto police; PW Botha; Piet Koornhof; the then Minister of Plural Relations, Connie Mulder; and Koot Vorster of the Dutch Reformed Church. By confronting those representing the ruling hegemony the interviewer situates himself as a force in opposition to them;

2. a 'black' community leader in Crossroads is interviewed. However, despite this 'balance', we see a preponderance of 'white' leadership;

3. 'ordinary whites', for example, farmer Riaan Kriel; and a 'poor white' urban Afrikaner trade unionist;

4. 'ordinary blacks', for example, a migrant worker in a 'city' hostel, his family in the homelands; a middle class doctor; an urban worker and his family in a location 'hovel'.

5. Totally absent, are 'white' English-speaking 'Captains of Industry'.

An analysis of the above cross-section of 'blacks' shows that they are always portrayed as victims of the Afrikaner. The mode of discourse thus creates a viewer who identifies with the British point of view, thereby creating a collusion of 'Us' against the Afrikaner 'Them'. This articulation conceals the historic struggles of 'blacks' against the English-Afrikaner hegemony of the state.

The verbal codes are supported by other codes of film-making - but always to enlist our humanist support - for both sides. Music is used to create atmosphere: the playing of **Die Stem** when the military/political might of the State is depicted; silence when a newsreel of police shooting students is shown. Black and white photographs, newsreel and films are used to show events in the past: the Battle of Blood River and the 1976 "massacre" of 'blacks' during the school boycotts and disturbances. Thus, the viewer's sympathies are for both 'white' and 'black' victims of violence.

Cinematic Style

Cinematographic codes and the cinéma vérité documentary style are used to endorse the film's authenticity and contemporaneity. The viewer is thus treated to many sequences of the director-cum-interviewer driving out to remote places to interview people and collect the raw data of his enquiry. Of significance is the way in which he is brought into focus and close up every time he asks a 'leading' question. The effect of this camera action is to display the interviewer. We are thus shown democratic capitalism - symbolised by Dimbleby - confronting the forces of oppression. The implication is that capitalism and the forces of oppression are mutually exclusive categories: the myth. Thus, despite the exposé of a misguided group, the film-maker recreates the myth of liberal capitalism. Indeed, Seth Feldman (1977) raises the issue of who we should consider as the subject of documentary films, and he suggests that at some point in the future, the Worth-Adair Navajo films might be thought to be more about the state of American anthropology, than the Navajo. Similarly, **The White Tribe of Africa** is more of an index of the nature of British libertarianism than it is about the 'white' tribe in Africa.

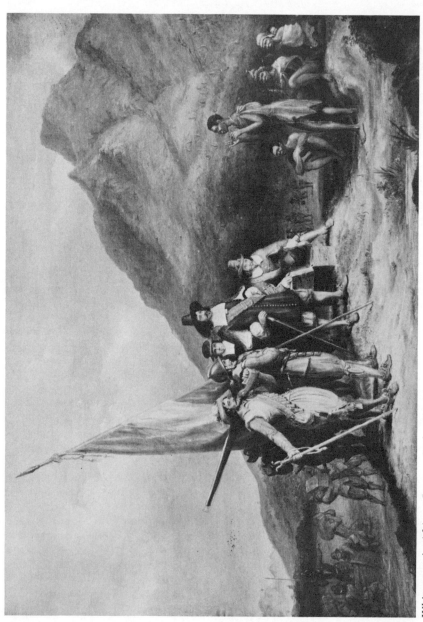

White roots in Africa – Jan van Riebeeck.

From the above analysis of **The White Tribe in Africa,** one can see how objective reality is viewed from a particular stance - the gaze of the dominant ideology within the British state - which thereby controls the 'gaze within the series'. This particular mode of discourse closes off other interpretations of South African reality and produces a monologue in which the illusion is created that the observer and observed exist in different worlds. This discourse exemplifies Paul Rotha's (1936:134) statement that "Most documentary is only truthful in that it represents an attitude of mind".

THE STRUGGLE FOR THE SIGN

Those who are the object of the gaze in the British production are not powerless. They too have documentary film which they can use to communicate their version of 'reality'. Thus the films, **To Act a Lie, A Place Called Soweto, White Roots in Africa, The Solution to the Dilemma of a Plural Society,** and so on become part of a salvo in the struggle for the appropriation of images by which South Africa could be/is represented.

The intentions of **To Act a Lie** are clear: to counter the image of South Africa represented in films by "various anti-South African producers who are pirating the South African scene". **To Act a Lie** sets out to accomplish two particular tasks: to look at film as images of reality, questioning their relation to that reality; and to create an impression of reality (the 'true reality', as opposed to the 'false reality' of hostile film-makers) by presenting images of the 'real' South Africa.

The task appears contradictory, but the director of **To Act a Lie** tries to solve the 'problem' of foreign misrepresentation by using two distinct codes: colour and black and white photography. Monochromatic photography is used to connote the distorted imagery or visual lies of foreign film-makers; colour photography is used to denote 'truth' or 'reality'. Thus a single code has been split so that one aspect of it represents 'image', and the other, 'reality'. The implications of this intellectual juggling is that the director is trying to draw a visual distinction between 'true' and 'false' images as though they were mutually exclusive categories,

To Act a Lie/A Place Called Soweto.

thus denying the single concept 'image' as one which is informed by a particular ideology.

Using elaborated codes from film, the narrator castigates anti-South African film-makers for the:

> wilful deception through the exploitation of subjects and set-up scenes which has made a mockery of the techniques of filming and editing which were once the stock-in-trade of documentary film-making.

By acknowledging "techniques of filming and editing", the film-makers are acknowledging cinematic practice. More specifically, they are acknowledging that the cinema is an intervention into 'reality' which necessitates a mediating ideology, and not simply a recording of reality. However, having made this assertion vis-a-vis anti-South African films, they then proceed to construct a film which both denies ideology, attempting to present image as reality; and simultaneously use the very "techniques of filming and editing" which they have discredited.

The debate about image and reality is presented in two codes: voice-over narration and words on the screen. The text quoted in the previous paragraph is rolled up the screen with white lettering on a black background. As we see these signs appear, we hear a newscaster-type voice reading the words. The inflection of his voice connotes that what audiences will hear will be the 'truth', impartial and informed. Then follow the titles of the anti-South African films, for example, **Apartheid: Twentieth Century Slavery, The End of Dialogue, The Defiant White Tribe,** and finally, **Last Grave at Dimbaza.** The camera zooms into a close-up of this last title and metaphorically stamps across it in red and yellow lettering: **To Act A Lie.** Drums roll and a symbol clashes, indicating the beginning of our 'drama'.

Music is an unobtrusive code, but it is very effectively used in **To Act a Lie.** Apart from informing us subliminally of the direction that a particular sequence will take, the music also provides the continuity between visually different sequences and breaks in the voice-over.

However, the prime function seems to be within sequences: the kind of music indicates the kind of reaction we should have to a particular diegetic sequence. The eerie electronic music indicates the 'subversive', 'clandestine' and 'untrue' nature of the monochromatic film of the anti-South African film-makers, thereby signalling that we should reject such alien discourses. In contrast, the sophisticated night club jazz is bright and engaging, thus inviting the audience to participate in the particular diegetic sequence.

The use of the musical code is just one of the "techniques" of film-making which is the stock-in-trade of documentary film-making" described by the narrator of **To Act a Lie.** Film music is one of the most ideologically laden codes, as most audiences are not consciously aware of listening to the music. Thus, whatever music they do hear while watching a film, is deemed to be 'obvious'/'natural' for the particular sequence.

Music is used in conjunction with two other codes: visual codes and voice-over narration. Each of these has an internal logic which is cleverly constructed, and they cohere to create 'cinema'. Thus, there is a constant interplay between codes, so that the voice-over might end on, or emphasise a particular word, which becomes the entry point to the next visual sequence. An example of this is the sequence dealing with opportunities for 'blacks'. The following voice-over presents a God's-eye view: "if he's lucky he grows up only to collect garbage bags in the back alleys of white suburbs or to work in the kitchens of white South Africans", which introduces the visual sequence which shows, in colour, a typing class/business studies class/modelling (at this point the sophisticated jazz music starts)/a 'black' businessman dealing with a client show-jumping/horse-racing - 'black' jockey/beauty competition/a jazz group playing the music that we have been hearing/ballroom dancing/bar scene. It must be noted that the voice-over stops during the sequence, there seems to be a 'silence', except for the unobtrusive music. The effect of this interweave of codes is that the visual predominates: we are left alone to see for ourselves - and in this way ideology is denied: images parade as 'reality'.

The 'principle' of 'see with your own eyes' is also exemplified in **A Place Called Soweto,** where we are taken into the township on what appears to be a 'fact-finding mission'. As in **To Act a Lie,** the fallacy is that of the medium: that what we see is 'real'. However, we should remember that what is visible on the screen are signifiers, iconic signs which resemble their referents, not the signifieds themselves.

Two kinds of verbal codes are used: the 'anonymous' narration of the Voice of Authority, knowledge, impartial truth (the codes of the newscasting voice), and the assigned voices of 'people in the community who should know'. Their blackness (icon) makes them of the 'black' community, but their class position (bourgeois and petty bourgeois) puts them in a very different relation to the mass of 'blacks' and to capital. Thus, as icons they are supposed to be seen as metonyms for all 'blacks', but indexically the image conveys the idea of smoothly functioning racial capitalism. Another assigned voice is that of Dr Chris Barnard (who also appears in **White Roots in Africa**). As a world renowned heart surgeon he functions indexically as the authority on medicine and health affairs, but he also functions in the kind of way that film stars do: recognition and familiarity reassure the viewer. His presence thus seems 'natural'. He is seen as 'reality', a signified, and not as 'image', or signifier. In this way the ideological reasons for his appearance on the screen are not questioned.

Each of the interviewees is used to convey a particular relation between the verbal and visual codes, and this must be seen in relation to the overall construction of the film. The text is a very tightly constructed argument which is based on five premises. Firstly, that films present images of reality. These images can be manipulated to distort reality. Proof of this is presented by Mr Justice Tshungu, television and radio personality who describes a Dutch television presentation of a debate between himself and the SWAPO president. He notes that: "this indeed surprised me very greatly, that an image which I was party to the previous day could change in such a great way that I could not recognise it the next day".

Secondly, anti-South African films present false images of reality (shown in the visual code by monochromatic film). Thirdly, the 'anonymous' authoritative voice deals with the false (negative) image of reality, and is treated as 'image'. This relates to what South Africa's detractors say, and has a 'linear' relation to the

Future Roots. – *Subsistence agriculture in Ciskei.*

Scene of mine lift in Future Roots. It shows mine workers as mere cyphers in the capital accumulation process whereby they are merely paid sufficient wages to reproduce themselves.

black and white visual code which portrays these 'false images'. However, fourthly, this voice also has a 'contrapuntal' relation to the 'true' visual images - in colour - of South Africa which the film presents. Thus the film proceeds in a 'staggered' fashion: voice-over about 'false images' said in a cynical and supercilious tone of voice which seems to scoff at the 'false images', while it smugly illustrates the 'true images', so that the viewer ends up watching a verbal-visual irony.

Finally, the assigned voices proceed from the 'black' signifiers who represent examples of the positive image of South Africa. These verbal and visual colour codes thus work in concert to present 'reality'. The film-maker would, in these sequences, deny the image aspect of film, thus employing "techniques of film-making and editing" which give the impression of reality, thereby denying the presence of the ideology of the film-makers.

Having clarified the formal position from which the film is made, attention is given to the content of the argument. Again, this proceeds logically and it is apparent that a lot of thought has gone into the script: another textual dimension in which ideology intervenes. The film unfolds by dealing with the various 'issues' dealt with in anti-South African films. These include the land question, housing, education, 'black' development, health care, and homeland independence. We can now move to a more detailed analysis of the diegetic sequences which portray the various elements of the 'argument' we have described.

Having introduced the idea that foreign films present 'lies', by the camera zoom in on the title **To Act A Lie** stamped over the title of an anti-South African film, **Last Grave at Dimbaza,** the film then opens with a black and white sequence showing shots from these films. We see a close-up of a grave "of a black child ... whom a pirate producer ... rigged or true?" intones the voice-over. The commentary does not deal with the signifier, that is, with what relation the image has to reality, it simply denies the existence of a signified and tackles the way in which "pirating producers have stripped the black man of his dignity before the audiences of the world". The director thus sets himself up as the presenter of the 'dignity' of the 'black' man. The film purports to speak for the 'black' person in South Africa, in contrast to the anti-South African film-makers who have 'exploited' the 'black' person by appropriating images of them as "hewers of wood or poor uneducated labourers". The implication is that the film will present the 'real' 'black' person in South Africa, not the clichéd poverty-stricken African, but ... The camera then cuts to a colour sequence in a 'black' supermarket, where well-dressed people are shopping. The music is bright and jazzy and suggests energy and action. The camera is also on the move, reinforcing this sense of dynamism and contemporaneity. This is in stark contrast to the previous black and white sequence in which we saw a series of static, poor quality shots which gave the impression of having been taken from the archives, or of having been clandestinely shot - casting doubt on the legitimacy of the footage.

The film then proceeds to 'debunk' some of the myths presented by foreign film-makers. The most important issue, the land question is dealt with first. This is crucial to any analysis of South African politics, for it is the focal point regarding the legitimacy of 'white' hegemony in the country. We are introduced to this sequence, first by electronic 'space' music, and we then see an icon of the globe spinning in space as the camera then zooms into South Africa on the globe, while the voice-over informs us that "indubitably part of this world, the Republic of South Africa, is a microcosm ..." of the world, but that certain film-makers have only presented the negative side. "Part of this world" is a key phrase, because South Africa is constantly being boycotted by the rest of the world for its apartheid policies. However, the portrayal of negative images is followed by a juxtaposition of shots showing a woman and a child walking down the road - in dreadful quality black and white film - with a shot of a 'multiracial' party in which sophisticated-looking women are elegantly dressed. The music becomes jazzy and alive and there is rapid cutting to icons of a clover leaf road system, harbour, SAA jet taking off, and so on. The voice-over describes the stature of South Africa: "Ranked among the 20 most developed nations of the world and the only truly industrialised state on the African continent, aligned with the West and avowedly inseparable from its African heritage ...", yet it is this state that is singled out and castigated for its policies. This is a classic sequence in which the voice-over provides the negatives of which South Africa has been accused, while the visual code provides the positive images. For example: "poor health service", over shot of medical technology and patient whose temperature is being taken; "starvation wages" over a picture of a 'black' bank or building society teller and customers; "denial of human rights" over a 'black' lawyer in a courtroom; "hovel-like housing" over a shot of a businessman leaving a grand house and climbing into a posh car; "keeping the black man from advancing" over shots of a 'black' man driving a tractor.

Finally, everything "negative" is said to be "lumped under one word - apartheid", and we see a boardroom meeting of 'black' and 'white' men. The camera zooms in on the 'black' man who is talking - indexical of his control. Despite the fact that the camera very nonchalantly seems to be finding these scenes as if by accident, the formal act of zooming in betrays the presence of the film-maker - a sign for the observant amongst the audience that what the film-maker reveals can be no more than an image. The particular images chosen are supposed to be metonyms, but they are, in fact, the exceptions which have been singled out for display.

The sequence started with an icon of the globe; the camera zoomed into South Africa. It is shown in its "plurality", as the "microcosm" of the world. These early shots thus provide a context in which the land question is raised:

> Anti-South African detractors say that 87% of the country is reserved for white occupation and a mere 13% for black occupation ... This quantitative instead of qualitative summing up disregards the fact that a vast area of South Africa consists of mountains and semi-desert terrain where only a few white people have managed to eke out a living and where no black man wants to live or has lived in the past - let alone staking a claim to the land.

This commentary coincides with a map of South Africa on which first the mountains, then a wet coastal strip, and then black marking representing industrialised areas are demarcated. The narration informs viewers that "only 100 000 square kilometers of the coastal strip has a wet temperate climate and that half of this is owned by blacks, and that the industrialised areas cut across both 'white' and 'black' land, all of which makes nonsense of the critics' argument that 87% is 'white' owned, and only 13% is 'black' owned". This explanation tries to rationalise the existing land distribution. However, the explanation - the mapping of description onto tautology - contains only the information present in the description. The employment of this quasi-scientific method testifies to the film-maker's need to challenge alternative views regarding the distribution of land. (The land sequence is a recurring element in state propaganda films and is presented with varying degrees of accuracy/falsity. See Tomaselli, (1980b:13) for a brief analysis of **Solution to the Dilemma of a Plural Society**).

Education is another issue dealt with in the film. Once more the narration which represents Authority, Objectivity and Knowledge is used to introduce the sequence, providing the negative image of South Africa presented by foreign film-makers: "a popular state-ment is that by law, blacks unlike whites have to pay for their children's education, and that it is inferior". The director then cuts to a mid long shot and then a mid close-up of the Rector of the University of the North sitting in a very spacious and opulent office. He then proceeds to introduce himself and describe his professional qualifications (5 degrees) which "I owe entirely to the facilities that have been provided for black people within this country". This is said over descriptive panning shots of the campus, showing its magnificent modernity, interior shots showing students working, the library and so on. The voice-over and the icon are used to provide a living example of educational opportu-nities for 'blacks' in South Africa. The way in which he is dis-played and the extensive colour shots of the campus testify to the up-to-dateness of the proof. Once more, this particular example is used as a metonym for the educational opportunities for all 'blacks'. However, as John Fiske (1982:98) notes:

> The arbitrariness of this selection is often disguised or at least ignored, and the metonym is made to appear a natural index and thus is given the status of 'the real', and 'not the unquestioned'.

It is Fiske's contention that the selection of a metonym from a given paradigm, although 'arbitrary', is based on the cultural value or myth that the communicator wishes to present. This principle is seen time and again in state propaganda films. In **A Place Called Soweto,** for example, it is evident in the sequences which deal with technical education, hospital services, child care, sport and commerce.

To Act A Lie ends with a sequence which deals with the "plurality" of South African society. The authoritative voice-over informs us that "South Africa has a society so complex and interwoven, that by emphasising the negative, without showing South Africa's other image, makes any producer guilty of political and intellectual dishonesty". Then follows a montage of shots showing a busy urban street scene with 'black' and 'white' pedestrians, a 'black' graduation ceremony, and tribal dances. These are icons of the "other image" of South Africa which oppositional film-makers have ignored. However, given that the premise on which these images function is metonymic, we can see that the producer is also guilty of "intellectual dishonesty".

The portrayal of South Africa as a "plural society" "composed of twelve different ethnic groups, all within a common frontier, each with a state in the country, each with its own identity and parti-cular characteristics and political aspirations ..." is the basis of the argument regarding 'black' citizenship in South Africa. Thus, by providing 'blacks' with "states" within South Africa, the film is able to rationalise the denial of the franchise and citizenship to 'black' South Africans. The viewer is treated to a visual display of "independence celebrations" with much pomp and military ceremony (also seen in other films like **Venda: 'n Nuwe Staat**). The authoritative narration informs viewers that:

> The world has seen devastating wars in which blood flowed for the sake of independence and freedom. Without spilling a drop of ink to sign away freedom and independence to two of its black nations so far, South Africa has set an example which is still out of reach of the United Nations.

This is a rather crude way of getting at the United Nations, an in-ternational forum through which official international opposition to South Africa is lodged. The final image of South Africa we are left with is of BJ Vorster and President Matanzima shaking hands. This shot is frozen, and the film ends, leaving the viewer with the clasped hands: an index of the success of the 'separate but equal' discourse of apartheid.

Despite the apparently discursive nature of the text, and the way in which it tries to deal with both film-as-image, and image-as-reality, it ends in a very positive way as both verbal and visual codes cohere. The concluding sequence is presented as a concluding statement in a court of law, and the voice chosen for this sequence is the Voice of Authority:

"... the exploitation of subjects to create the impression of blacks as only hewers of wood ... is ... TO ACT A LIE."

"... to portray the black man as a person stripped of his rights is TO ACT A LIE."

"... to portray the granting of independence to black nations as cosmetic is ... TO ACT A LIE."

The repetition of the words "to act a lie" is a reinforcement of the original icon on the screen, and one can almost hear the thud as the Voice of Authority stamps this message on the viewer's consciousness. Here, the verbal code is supported by colour images of 'blacks' succeeding in various spheres. Thus, we are left with a double negative which leaves the audience in no doubt as to what the 'real' situation in South Africa is. The ultimate irony is that these 'blacks' are signifiers, not signifieds, and as such are NOT metonyms for all 'black' South Africans. They are the bourgeois and petty bourgeois exceptions which racial capitalism creates in order to reproduce itself. As the 'black' people in the film are signifiers, they are images of reality, and thus if the film purports to portray 'reality' in South Africa then it is doing so "TO ACT A LIE".

Presence/Absence of English-Speaking South Africans

In **The White Tribe of Africa,** "white" is synonomous with 'Afrikaner', and the social and political history of South Africa is interpreted from this false premise. Thus Afrikaners become the scapegoat for all that is wrong in South Africa.

The equation of 'white' with 'Afrikaner' is correctly challenged by producers working under the auspices of the Department of Information - a government body - and as such they represent the National Party point of view. In a film like **To Act a Lie,** the challenge is directed at the epithet, 'racist', that is applied to Afrikaners. The film thus tries to show how much the South African government does for 'blacks'.

'Blacks' thus become the object of the gaze in South African state - to prove the falseness of the image of Afrikaners presented by series such as **The White Tribe of Africa.** In order to achieve what is logically impossible, **To Act a Lie** operates using the exceptional case, so that as signifiers they appear to function metonymically.

In a film such as **White Roots in Africa,** a different approach is used. Here, semantics and false logic are employed to present 'whites' in South Africa. The film shifts between talking about the English and Afrikaners when in fact, it is presenting a history of capital on the sub-continent. Terms such as 'English', 'Afrikaner', 'white people', 'ethnic national groups', 'Asians', 'Indian community', 'coloured', 'brown', 'black', 'nation states', 'our peoples' and 'population communities' are used to present a multiplicity of differences in the people and their relation to the state and the South African economy. However, when the economy is described, then the possessive adjective "our" is used by National Party spokesmen or men who represent industrial or finance capital. It is in this context that "unity", "collaboration" and "togetherness" are used, and in this context that the narration challenges foreign misconceptions: "The white man is often described as a racist ... bible puncher ... member of the defiant white tribe of Africa". What was a structured absence in **The White Tribe of Africa** - the English-speaking 'white' South Africans - becomes subsumed under "white" in **White Roots in Africa.** English-Afrikaner unity is presented as being achieved through 'culture', which is defined in relation to 'civilisation' and is embodied in such practices as ballet, and classical orchestra music as opposed to the structured absence, the 'primitive', as represented by 'black' cultural practices. Thus these practices by definition become 'white': 'black' ballet is inconceivable (this argument also applies to **South Africa's Performing Arts).**

Conclusion

From an analysis of the above-mentioned films and television series it becomes apparent that each is a monologue, an attempt to portray and 'explain' the South African 'reality'. They go much further than ethnographic films which attempt to reveal, describe and portray cultures in relation to written anthropology or other body of knowledge, rather than in relation to the political criticisms repetitively articulated in the world's mass media. Neither is the explanation offered in the above films 'reality' or 'true', whether of the South African or the British variety. As Bill Nichols (1982:266) notes:

> Explanation operates at a remove, at a different logical ty-ping. Hence explanation, like a map, is not the territory. There is a gap between it and the observable phenomena, the pro-filmic event it sets out to explain, a gap that can act as a fissure in the indexial sign. This gap involves recognition of the sense in which there is more to understanding a situation or event than meets the eye (either in terms of the cinematic apparatus and the production of meaning or the event and its attendant explanation).

Thus it is evident that the documentary, even when infused with ethnographic discourse such as 'tribe', 'community', 'peoples' and 'roots', do not guarantee 'truth', despite the fact that its signi-fiers are taken from objective (ideologically determined) reality. There is no unique, one-to-one relation between signifiers and signifieds. The film-maker produces a discourse which identifies and positions the viewer in a particular way, so that a preferred reading of the discourse is encoded into the text. However, in the process of semiosis the viewer decodes the text in relation to a theoretical and ideological matrix which is distinct from any specific observation or views presented in the text. The way in which the text is both encoded and decoded will depend on the fit between pre-existent views and the observations presented. Nichols (1981:267) sees the fit as being "governed by the principle of tautology when scrutinized formally, and by the principle of purpose when examined contextually". Thus, 'truth' can be traced by the relation between text and purpose, rather than pre-ordained absolutes. Indeed, it is by scrutinising purpose, founded upon historical and ideological imperatives, that one may approach 'truth'.

All of the films and television series discussed in this chapter dis-play a marginal degree of ethnographic understanding about the so-

cieties which they are respectively trying to expose. Their
intentions are propagandistic, their purposes are propagandistic.
What separates the South African films from the British television
series rests on the consciousness of technique and form. Where
The White Tribe of Africa merely glides along within the
conventions of the television documentary, the South African films
question those conventions either implicity or explicitly, and then
offer a series of counter-signs and codes to discredit the foreign
interpretation, while using the conventions of structured propaganda documentary.

The struggle is not over ethnographic or anthropological understanding, it is a political struggle over the appropriation of cultural images.

CHAPTER FIVE

THE 'BUSHMEN' ON FILM:
FROM COLONIALISM TO ROMANTICISM

INTRODUCTION

This chapter provides an overview of films dealing with the 'bushmen', generally known as the San or !Kung, in Southern Africa. The films range from naive or propagandistic ethnographic film to more sophisticated descriptive realism. The earliest example is the **Denver Africa Expedition** (also known as **The Bushmen**), produced in 1912. It was a collaborative effort between the Universities of Denver and Cape Town, and the South African Museum. The most recent documents considered here are the television series, **Testament to the Bushmen** and John Marshall's film, **N!ai: The Story of a !Kung Woman.**

The selection of films for ethnographic analysis was based primarily on their availability. Only half the films were made by South Africans. The remainder were either produced by foreigners or as collaborative efforts for both national and international distribution (eg. **Testament to the Bushmen).** This chapter will include a consideration of the overriding themes common to certain clearly identified groups of film.

ANTHROPOLOGICAL UNDERSTANDING

In the main, most films on the San deal with the 'spectacular' or anomalous aspects of 'Bushmen' cultures and do not contribute to holistic understanding. These films nevertheless constitute important ethnographic documents. They allow us to make inferences about a specific colonial ideology that was pervasive at the time as well as to see specific sequences dealing with certain rituals, social behaviour or artifacts in historical perspective. For example, we are able to compare social behaviour as mediated through the films of the early part of this century with contemporary accounts and use the comparison as an index of change in the anthropological understanding of the San. Existing ethnographic film theory therefore, is only partly able to account for these unintentional and naive ethnographic films. Karl Heider (1983) has offered a compromise approach to the problem of "scholastic exclusiveness" of contemporary views on ethnographic film. He suggests that while a consideration of the attributes of ethnographic film might be meaningful to

> other anthropologists who already have a good idea of what ethnography is all about ... to others it is hardly a helpful definition for ethnography itself is a fuzzy category and attempts at definition of the field tend to be fatuous (Heider, 1983:2).

Heider re-asserts the broad elements of ethnographic film which includes a theoretically based analysis; emersing oneself in the subject community for a period of observation which is then translated onto film. Recognising that the concept of truth is problematic in that it remains a goal of the social sciences yet it is always mediated through a subjective process, he suggests that a reassessment is necessary to overcome this paradox:

> I mean that 'truth' and 'neutrality', as absolutes, are not words that start arguments. The arguments we do have ultimately revolve around questions of which paradigm is the most useful; which accounts for the most important data and loses the least; and which has more desirable degree of truth or neutrality (Heider, 1983:2).

To the 'exclusivist' ethnographic film theorists, this may constitute an unacceptable compromise but for our purposes it is the only viable way of taking account of problematic categories of film which broadly match up to the criteria of ethnographic film being "about people" (Heider, 1972) or "which seeks to reveal one society to another" (MacDougall, 1969:16). While accepting that the more uncompromising approaches characteristic of the descriptive realism of 'cinema verite' or 'observational cinema' is necessary for the laying of guidelines for future production, they do nothing to assist in a **post hoc** analysis of films where the specific ethnographic intentions of the producer are questionable.

Heider's revised paradigm includes three broad categories. Firstly there is "Descriptive Realism", where events tend to speak for themselves and where non-interventionist practices are favoured. According to Richard Leacock (1971:6), one of the pioneers of cinema verite:

> We ... subjected ourselves to a rather rigid set of rules. If we missed something, never asked anyone to repeat it. Never ask any questions. Never interview. We rarely broke them (the rules) and when we did we regretted it.

The approach is a radical one and discounts much contemporary ethnographic film which is still tied to documentary conventions by an umbilical cord of interpretive, interventionist practices.

Heider's second category of "Interpretive Realism" is characterised by a "methodological delicacy that is lacking in most ethnographic films, where the imposition of a theoretical framework is more obvious" (Heider, 1983:6). The "imposition" is defined by Heider as an attempt to impose order on reality which he sees as the function and essence of all science. On the face of it, it would appear that interpretive realism is the very antithesis of descriptive realism but, as Heider points out, "the two must be seen, not as opposed categories, but as opposite ends of a continuum". While accepting his continuum thesis, efforts to place the films considered for this study into that continuum, show that the continuum itself has fundamental limitations. For one, it is clear that Heider's two basic premises are an understanding of the anthropological discipline as well as an **intention** to construct the visual codes in a film so as to fit somewhere between observational cinema and interpretive documentary. Few of the films dealt with in this study appear to satisfy either of these criteria. For example, the subtitles in **Denver Africa Expedition** provide an interpretation (and hence satisfy the major criterion of interpretive realism), but the interpretation is trivial and wrong. Far from simply losing the opportunity to add to the fund of more routine ethnography (MacDougall, 1975:116), the films perpetuate the myth of the Noble Savage through a process of misinformation. Nevertheless, the film provides valuable historical ethnographic data on techniques of collecting water, hunting practices and dance. The value of these sequences, however, are only apparent once the sub-titles are removed, resulting in an undercoded text from which anthropologically useful inferences can be made. It is the **lack** of intention that makes them valuable as historical ethnographic documents if studied in the context in which they were produced.

A third category is "Native Realism" where the subject group describes their own culture. This is an optimistic look into the future and approximates Worth's Navajo Project. It throws up its own specific issues which do not fall within the ambit of this study. Other than **I am Clifford Abrahams: This is Grahamstown,** we are aware of no other South African attempt to even begin to breach the dichotomy between production practices which distinguish films **of** culture from films **about** culture.

Heider's continuum can be used for the criticism of contemporary ethnographic film and can be applied as guidelines for the production of future films. However, the continuum thesis does not account for the anomalous category of the historically important and ethnographically relevant area into which most of the early films on the San fit. It is therefore necessary to extend the continuum to include various sub-categories. "Naive Ethnographic Film" is one such category (Van Zyl, 1980a) and includes those films which manifest isolated yet valuable ethnographic information. Films to be included in the naive ethnography category are **Denver Africa Expedition** and **Remnants of a Race** (there is also an Afrikaans version called **Swerwers van die Sandveld**). Much of the content of these films can be dismissed as colonial propaganda or as having secondary importance only inasmuch as they expose early 20th century British paternal ethnocentrism or racism. Following Heider (1972) this alone is a sufficient criterion for considering these films as ethnographic documents.

Another category which is clearly discernable in the films on the San is one which may be termed 'Instructional Ethnographic Film'. Instructional films are those which appear to have been made specifically for the classroom situation. Films in this category are characterised by decontextualisation and fragmentation of reality. They include **Boesman Boogmaker, Kalahari Klaskamer,** and **Rock Art Treasures.** They manifest elements of interpretive realism insofar as the narration seeks to clarify or explain the visual. They also manifest some of the elements of misinformation and ideological distortion characteristic of naive ethnographic films.

THE LEGACY OF FILM ON THE SAN

Naive Ethnographic Film

Denver Africa Expedition (1912) is one of the first films to deal with the San. The credits cloak the film in a guise of academic respectability which belies its crass and hackneyed content. The film makes a wide and confusing sweep of southern African traditional culture. By doing so the film fails to indicate any cultural differences between the groups of people it documents in the sub-continent. The obvious characteristic that thematically binds these diverse groups and tribes together is the darker colour of their skins and their alleged 'barbaric' forms of existence. It is only halfway through that we get a specific consideration of the Bushmen. There is a distinctly colonial flavour to the narrative discourse. The subtitles are ethnocentric in the extreme and the notion of a voyage into Humankind's romanticised past where 'what we were' is juxtaposed with 'what we are', or have become. Predictably, Western culture is projected as the end point in the progression from 'savagery' to 'civilization'.

The British colonialist tradition is maintained through an overt and thoroughly unsubtle process of highlighting those elements with which the viewership 'back home' would identify. References are made to Africa as "the Mother of all Living", and Nairobi as "an inland outpost of Britain's farflung battle line".

Denver African Expedition manifests a 'zoo ethos' where the viewer is implicitly encouraged to sit back and watch while the film unfolds the 'magic of Africa' using traditional culture as an ideosyncratic vehicle to achieve this. On occasion this 'zoo ethos' takes on a more overtly racist character. In one sequence where the expeditionary party have finally made contact with the "elusive little yellow men", we see a member of the party placing offerings on a Bushman trail in an effort to lure them out of hiding. The methods used to entice baboons out of hiding serve equally well for the Bushmen. In **Remnants of a Race,** produced in 1940, the 'zoo ethos' is taken to its most racist conclusion where the narration states:

> if you are lucky enough you are rewarded by the sight of the little primitive men you are looking for. And if you do see

him, he'll give you the opportunity to make close contact and thus allow you to take those rare pictures you're so anxious to get.

Here, the Bushmen are quite unsubtly likened to wild animals. They are elusive at best and dangerous at worst.

Traditional culture, whether of the San or Zulu, is portrayed as being quaint. Aspects of traditional culture are given prominence only insofar as they are counter-balanced with an equivalent aspect of Western culture and where those equivalent aspects of traditional culture can be ridiculed as a result of the comparison. In neither of the films is traditional culture seen to be of any relevance in and of itself.

There is no overt missionary-type zeal to try and civilize traditional groups in **Denver Africa Expedition** or **Remnants of a Race**. Both films present traditional culture in as naked a way as early 20th century film aesthetics would allow and then attempt to ridicule or trivialise those selected aspects by virtue of their juxtaposition with Western 'civilized' standards.

In an analysis of the Noble Savage in literature dealing specifically with the San, Wright (1983) indicates that early 20th century literature "(had begun) a process of rehabilitating the San in the eyes of the societies which all but destroyed them, and which can now, ... afford to pity and even romanticize them" (Wright, 1983:61). Wright indicates that there is a direct correlation between a particular ideology pervasive at a specific juncture in the colonial history of South Africa and the subsequent literary or filmic treatments of the San. An analysis of **Denver Africa Expedition** and **Remnants of a Race** shows that the colonial ideology may be adapted from literature and transposed almost directly for the purposes of studying the San filmicly.

In a historical analysis of racial stereotypes in South Africa, Shula Marks has attributed the tendency to romanticize traditional culture like the San to the fact that "the San played a less and less important role in southern African affairs from the 19th century onward, until, by the end of the century they had become of marginal concern to the much more numerous white and Bantu-speaking population" (Marks, 1981:1). It is necessary to extend Marks' observations to include a materialist understanding of the economic reasons behind this tendency to romanticise the San in literature and film. In a comparative analysis of the concept of the Noble Savage as it applied to the North American Indian and African, as well as subsequent attempts to civilize them, Winthrop Jordan (1974:15) states:

> ... the savagory of the Indians assumed a special significance in the minds of those actively engaged in a program of bringing civilization into the American wilderness. The case with the African was different: the English errand into Africa was not a new or a perfect community but a business trip. No hope was entertained for civilizing the Negro's steaming continent, and Englishmen lacked compelling reason to develop a program for remodelling the African natives.

Although Jordan is referring specifically to the slave trade, this economic reasoning can be equally applied to early twentieth century filmic treatments of the San. From historical accounts of both black and white economic exploitation of San environmental resources, it appears that at the turn of the century either the San had little to offer, or they were numerically insignificant. Both reasons would explain why the San posed little threat to black and white economic or pastoral expansionists and why literature and film could afford to romanticize them. In **Denver Africa Expedition** and **Remnants of a Race** then, the tendency is to accept traditional culture as a given and to use it to humorous effect in an effort to reaffirm the superiority of Western civilized culture.

The two films exemplify what Jordan calls, "an exercise in self-inspection by means of comparison". He goes on to state:

> The necessity of continuously measuring African practices with an English yardstick ... tended to emphasize the differences between the two groups, but it also made for heightened sensitivity to instances of similarity. ... the Englishman's ethnocentrism tended to distort his perception of African culture in two opposite directions ... to emphasize differences and condemn deviations from the English norm ... (and) to seek out similarities (where perhaps none existed) and to applaud every instance of conformity (Jordan, 1974:14).

An arbitrary selection of evidence in **Denver Africa Expedition** in support of this claim includes sequences dealing with competition and dance. In the former case the apparent lack of competitiveness is dealt with in an almost incredulous way and no attempt is made to place this phenomenon in a social or economic framework. Silberbauer (1981:177) states that the San social structure manifests an absence of hierarchy within which members might compete for status:

> Competitiveness is generally discounted. There are no competitive games, the high rate of circulation of material goods in the kinship context negates the concept of exclusively owned wealth ... Adherence to this doctrine (where the deity is owner of the world but has ordained that Humankind may use His resources for survival) is impossible if not controlled. Control is facilitated by maintaining a surplus of resources in relation to the needs of the human population (Silberbauer, 1981:250).

Because of the lack of any contextual explanation for the apparent absence of competition amongst the San, we must assume that the narration sees competition in relation to a Western free market capitalism which requires a specific kind of competition to survive. The film-maker sees this lack of competition amongst the San as an opportunity to condemn deviations from the Western norm.

There are, however, numerous sequences in both **Denver Africa Expedition** and **Remnants of a Race** which qualify for an analysis based on their importance as valuable historical ethnography. In **Denver Africa Expedition** the appropriate sequences, if considered purely in terms of the visual, are treated holistically insofar as the camera employs lengthy wide angle shots and reduces potential distortion by giving adequate 'film space' to each sequence. Similar valuable ethnographic footage can be found in **Remnants of a Race** where we see the San smoking, treating skins, collecting water, painting and constructing Springhare traps. However, in all but the sequence on a San male extracting liquid from the contents of the stomach of a recently slaughtered animal, the narration or subtitles serve to obfuscate the visual rather than clarify it. In another example, we see an informative and visually instructive sequence on a San male extracting water from the soil. The narration, however, detracts almost totally from the visual and tries to explain it in terms of the divine intervention of Mother Nature. The narration (captions) states: "Mother Nature provides for her most primitive children in their hour of need. You in the audience may shudder at the thought of drinking this water, but then you haven't really been thirsty".

In summary, the two films falling into the category 'naïve ethnography' have much to condemn them as frivolous documents reflecting colonial traditions of self-importance and ethnocentrism. Their value lies in a selected few sequences 'sans' narration. We have given due consideration to those elements of the category which are of value only inasmuch as they reflect a colonialist ideology and indirectly tell us about the culture of the film-maker.

Instructional Ethnographic Film

Instructional ethnographic films are those made with a classroom viewership in mind. The films that comprise this category include **Boesman Boogmaker, Kalahari Klaskamer,** and **Rock Art Treasures.** Of the three films, **Boesman Boogmaker** and **Kalahari Klaskamer** are the most simplistic with **Rock Art Treasures** exhibiting a vastly more complex, stylistic use of the camera. All three decontextualize elements of San culture from the wider social and economic matrix. The films provide technicist, or overly descriptive, recipelike explanations of the more novel and ideosyncratic aspects related to the problem of survival in a hostile environment. As with most of the films considered for this study, the San themselves are never given the opportunity to address the camera directly. On the few occasions that we hear them speaking, the characteristic clicks of their language are used to add to the 'spectacular'. Very often the narration is also dissociated from the real action on the screen.

Boesman Boogmaker produced by R Johnston in 1964, deals exclusively with the making of bows and arrows. The 'action' is staged from beginning to end and the narration provides no analysis. The activity is seen as quaint, with the San given patronising credit for their expertise. At no stage do we hear or see how hunting (of which bow and arrow making is a relatively minor part) fits into the San subsistence network. The film trivialises the environmental pressures on survival and suggests that the Bushmen live in a timeless existence. The film totally lacks contextualization, but the camera is not a 'tourist' or 'conquerer'. The description is clinical, dense and didactic.

Kalahari Klaskamer (1964), another R Johnston film, attempts to draw a direct correlation between a San child's socialization and the more formal, institutionalized aspects of Western education. This is done through a process of fragmenting San socialization into clearly demarcated areas of school, homework and play which are made to parallel Western formal educational categories.

Although the film fragments out specific areas for consideration, within these sequences there is a holistic treatment of content. We are shown how to build a hut, how to dig for roots and tubers, how to discern edible berries, how to store water in ostrich eggs and how the San have perfected the art of making friction fires. Like many of the films already mentioned these areas hold their own as specifically ethnographic analyses only once the narration is removed and supplemented with a more appropriate description.

Ultimately, **Kalahari Klaskamer** is a technicist description of a fragmented aspect of San existence, namely instruction which is decontextualised from its social context. The camera is mostly at eye-level and directs the viewers' gaze downwards at the Bushmen, emphasising the position of the audience as invisible voyeur. The film is constantly punctuated by fade-outs which was an acceptable convention at the time of the film's production, but has the effect of dissecting a holistic social experience. This not only isolates the aspect of education from the all-encompassing social context, but also divides up the various educational events from each other. There is thus a greater separation from the overall context in which San children learn to do things.

Rock Art Treasures (1970), produced by Killarney Films, is a slick stylistic treatment of rock painting. The film was made with extensive assistance from the SABC. While the film is visually pleasing, its aesthetics appear to be in inverse proportion to the ethnographic relevance of the content. In this regard, there is a constant interplay between shots of real life and their corresponding representation (mainly animals) on the rock face. In most cases this takes the form of camera dissolves from one to the other. This use of 'special effects' corresponds to Heider's distinction between "realistic cinema" and "impressionistic cinema", **Rock Art Treasures** adhering to the latter:

> ... realistic cinema uses long takes, wide angle shots, and deep focus while impressionistic cinema is characterised by montage, close-ups, and shallow focus. On the whole, ethnographic film has more use for the realistic tool kit (Heider, 1983:3).

Rock Art Treasures exhibits certain elements of the structured absences discourse discussed in Chapter Three. While a good deal of the content appears to be ethnographically correct, it is the 'lack' or incomplete treatment of sequences that is of concern. Apart from telescoping time and place through the use of dissolves which suggests that the 'art' is still actively practiced today, there is no attempt to differentiate between specifically San paintings and those done by other traditional cultures. Philip Tobias tells us, for example, that:

> Not only is rock art widely distributed, but it covers a great range of time ... Bushmen are known to have made the last rock paintings about a hundred years ago. In South Africa the rock paintings have commonly been referred to as "Bushmen" paintings, but there is little doubt that the rock art in southern Africa was produced by different population groups in the past (Tobias, 1978:57).

San rock art is simplistically interpreted by comparing it to Western formal art forms or by facile reference to San ethnography. Lewis-Williams (1983) points to the complex interpretations required to understand San rock art:

> There is ... a unity of concept in the apparently confused composition which depends on ... different principles which call for an appreciation of the ways in which the San artists worked with metaphors to produce subtle and complex commentaries on their religious beliefs. It was these key metaphors which gave coherence to their artists' whole cognitive system as well as to their art (1983:246-247).

Even under the all-embracing heading "Bushman" rock art, there

Rock Art Treasures.

are numerous clearly defined styles belonging to different areas, periods and people. They include the Formal School which is found from Zimbabwe and the northern part of Namibia down to the south-western Cape. The Dynamic School is a more lively and colourful art style found mainly in the Drakensberg and the eastern Cape. The other "schools" of rock art painting include the Cape Schematic School, a cruder rock art form found in the inland plateau region; and the Central African Schematic School found in Angola, Zambia and East Africa (Tobias, 1978:57-58). While it would be unreasonable to expect an in-depth academic treatment of the different art forms in the film, the simplistic cinematic treatment of these forms belies the complexity of their interpretation.

As with Friedberg's **They Came From the East,** the importance of **Rock Art Treasures** as an ethnographic film lies not so much in what is said (both in the narration and visually) but what is not said. The difference, however, is that in Friedberg's case the absences were strategically structured, making **They Came From the East** the more discursive and penetrating document.

Rock Art Treasures provides misinformation which is only apparent once a comparison with written ethnography is made. In an obvious attempt to place San art in a social and historical context, the narration states:

> The sense of individuality of these ancient people remained virtually undeveloped. Essentially nomadic, they owned nothing more than they could carry and thus the rock artists seldom portrayed their people singly ... Individuality was pre-empted by a sense of unique racial identity in which the total was more meaningful than the individual parts.

Here there are no less than three areas of misinformation. Firstly, the San appear to have no linguistic equivalent of ownership and very few, if any, goods and services are the sole right of the individual. Secondly, Tobias (1978:62) states that, in general, there appears to be no specific rule relating to the numeric representation of figures in paintings: "The figures are often lively and very active ... They occur singly, in groups or in large scenes - hunting, fighting, dancing, sitting, lying down, standing, walking or running."

Thirdly, the narration refers to the San as having a sense of unique racial identity. Here the San are portrayed as having had a coherent and almost academic understanding of their racial exclusiveness. Apart from some confusion over who, or what group of people actually constitute the 'Bushmen' (see Tobias, 1978:1), Silberbauer (1981:3) states that "these people had no unifying organization that would have fostered a sense of shared identity and a common name with which to express it. Lumping them together was the invention of outsiders ..."

Clearly the concerns of the producers of **Rock Art Treasures** lay with the perpetuation of the race-based romantic stereotype of an Age long lost but captured for eternity (and for the edification of the film-maker) on the rock face. The stylistic treatment serves to divorce depiction from explanation. The paintings are seen to have a history of their own which is divorced from historical social reality. In spite of this dislocation, the description of the Voice of Authority tries to locate the 'place' of the Bushmen in the hierarchy of civilization in terms of apartheid discourse.

Rock Art Treasures is, in fact, less of an ethnographic study than it is a cinematic sculpture. It does not exhibit the crude ideology of the films discussed above. Through a metaphorical device of showing cracks in the rock art paintings, this film suggests the ravages of time on San existence where previous films located them within a timeless continuum. However, the time element is mentioned only with regard to the rock paintings and cracks, rock movements and the erosion of paint and is not directly related to the San as human beings whose painting is the product of complex cultural expression.

Fragmentary Ethnographic Films

In the logical progression from naive ethnography to interpretive realism, 'fragmentary ethnographic films' constitute the beginning of a conscious attempt to adhere to the newly developed body of theory governing production. Film-makers in this category have a sophisticated understanding of the requirements of anthropology as well as the parameters of the discipline and have successfully converted this knowledge into piecemeal treatments of specific aspects of San culture.

N!ai, The Story of a !Kung Woman.

A Curing Ceremony.

The Hunters.

This category includes the eighteen short films made by John Marshall over twenty seven years of periodic contact with the !Kung and San Bushmen. They include **An Argument About a Marriage** dealing with a domestic quarrel between two males who claim the same woman as their wife; **Baobab Play, Children Throw Toy Assegais, Tug-of-War, Playing with Scorpions, Lion Game, The Melon Tossing Game,** all about the games children play; **Bitter Lemons** which deals with San music; **A Curing Ceremony** which considers San medicine and the role of healers in the social context; **Debe's Tantrum** and **The Wasp Nest** about a specific individual's belligerent behaviour; **A Group of Women** concerning collective mothering where several women support each other and share the nurturing role; **A Joking Relationship** in which a young woman and her great uncle indulge in flirtatious behaviour; **The Meat Fight** which shows the !Kung's ability to settle disputes in the absence of institutionalised authority structures; **Men Bathing** which is about the sexual banter and innuendo that goes with the occasional baths San males are able to have during the wet seasons; **A Rite of Passage** dealing with a ceremony after a boy has killed his first antelope; and **!Kung Bushmen Hunting Equipment** shows in detail all the pieces in the !Kung hunting kit. None of these individual films treat !Kung macro culture holistically but, as with some of the more naïve ethnographic films already discussed, there is a holistic treatment of whole acts or individual aspects of culture.

Marshall as anthropologist has maintained an ethnographic presence to varying degrees but not Marshall the film-maker. Shots depicting overtly camera conscious subjects have obviously been edited out or alternatively, Marshall spent sufficient time with the !Kung so as to make the presence of the camera the rule rather than the exception through intensive sociality.

Seth Reichlin and John Marshall have provided study guides to most of these short films but significantly they do not include any reflexive documentation on decisions made during the filming or editing process. The study guides serve to contextualize the whole act within the wider social and economic context in a fairly detailed anthropological way.

The eighteen films comprising this category have been extensively used in Marshall's most recent ethnographic film entitled **N!ai: The Story of a !Kung Woman.** This film will be dealt with in more detail later.

Interpretive Realism

Heider defines interpretive realism as those films which try to interpret behaviour, make that interpretation explicit and take responsibility for that interpretation (Heider, 1983:6). He has made the category sufficiently broad to include its more rigid proponents (Leacock, 1971; Rouch 1975) as well as those films which adopt a more recognisable interpretive approach. Three such films are **The Hunters, Bushmen of the Kalahari,** and **N!ai: The Story of a !Kung Woman** produced by John Marshall. Heider alludes to certain reservations or problems normally associated with the interpretive approach. It is our intention to use these together with his "Attributes of Ethnographic Film" (Heider, 1972:47-96) in making a comprehensive analysis of the films incorporated in this category.

Colin Young (1975) makes the distinction between "telling a story and showing us something". Although he is not explicit as to what "telling a story" entails, we can assume it follows a documentary-style emphasis on an authoritative narration and visual story line. The style allows for very little independent interpretation on the part of the viewer and "we are ... locked into a single argument. We inherit someone else's view of the subject (not always the film-makers') and are given a take-it-or-leave-it option" (Young, 1975:69).

By extension we can further assume that "showing us something" does not include a pre-packaged take-it-or-leave-it option, but through the visual presentation as well as through the jucidious use, or absence of a narration, the viewer is challenged to make independent interpretations. MacDougall's (quoted in Heider, 1983) specific reservation about the "telling a story" brand of interpretive realism is that the interpretation might eventually prove to be incorrect as a result of misinterpretation by the film-maker/producer or because of the dynamic and ever-changing nature of the subject matter normally of interest to ethnographers. Both Young and MacDougall would therefore argue that unless film concentrates more on observation than on interpretation, it is likely to unintentionally make its content redundant to varying degrees.

Laurens van der Post and Paul Bellinger's **Testament to the Bushmen** is a curious combination of both the 'telling a story' and the 'showing us something' brand of interpretive realism. The combination arises from a seemingly accurate visual exposition of San culture on the one hand, and a narration that is both an explanation (and thus support of the visual) and a personal interpretation by the central, authoritative narrator on the other hand. In this regard, it is necessary to consider the film from these two different perspectives because they satisfy two different but not necessarily incompatible components of interpretive realism.

As stated by narrator Van der Post, the film series is his own personal voyage and testament of a people he knew as a child. By his own admission, the film was designed to perform several functions. Firstly, he makes reference to his grandfather who was partially instrumental in the demise of the Bushmen following several massacres in the eastern Transvaal before he was born. He states that as a young boy he remembers making an entry in his diary promising he would one day return to the Bushmen and "beg their pardon for what had happened in the past". We must assume that the film is an attempt to do just that and a sense of overriding responsibility and remorse at their predicament is a consistent theme throughout the six part series. Van der Post's intense emotion is indicated in what he says, the inflections of his voice, facial expression and in constant use of metaphors of the Bible through which he tries to elevate the Bushmen to an almost divine and innocent status.

Secondly, Van der Post states that the film was intended to serve as a follow-up to a previous film he made in 1954 entitled **The Lost World of the Kalahari** which resulted in a renewed concern by the British government over the fate of the Bushmen. Bellinger uses extracts from Van der Post's earlier film to illustrate certain sequences in **Testament to the Bushmen.** Clearly, a comparison between the two films is intended to serve as an index of change in the San community.

The superior visual content and technical competence of this film stands out as an exception to many of the more recent films produced on the San. The film is true - in an accidental way perhaps - to some of Heider's most important attributes of ethnographic film, including holism, whole bodies in whole acts and contextualization. This is partly due to Bellinger's extensive experience as a news cameraman where long take and wide shots

A Testament to the Bushmen.

offer the best news coverage. In one sequence of **Testament to the Bushmen,** for example, we see children playing the Melon Tossing Game. While the narration provides the necessary explanation, analysis and contextualization, the length of the footage dealing exclusively with the game itself allows the reader to draw conclusions regarding the extent of social integration afforded by the game. Other themes in the film dealt with in a similar way include sequences on the educative value of games, such as stick throwing, which are taught to young children by adults, bead-making, the collection and use of tubers, collecting water from tree hollows, a hunt and the sharing of meat.

Testament to the Bushmen is tightly structured so that one sequence inevitably serves to introduce the next, the net result being a smooth flow of events and cultural information. A sequence of an old man teaching two young boys the complex process of constructing bird snares is followed by them arriving back at camp just in time for the evening meal. We see them being welcomed by the group and the interaction surrounding the meal functions as the basis for an in-depth visual treatment of such leisure activity as smoking and the making of toy dolls by the children. The continuity of sequences is reproduced within each episode throughout the series.

The continuity within each episode is, however, not duplicated between the six episodes, resulting in a fragmentation of real action into clearly defined and visually manageable episodic segments. These detract from the dynamic and complex interaction within the social group and between the individual, and social group and the environment.

The first episode is an introduction where Van der Post outlines the purpose behind the series, introduces the viewer to the San and sketches a historical background. The second episode is subtitled "Children of the Desert" ('children' is an unfortunate reference to the diminutive size of the San although it could be interpreted as a racist reference to their often perceived childlike intelligence) and deals with the problems associated with survival in the desert. Episodes Three and Four concentrate on the roles of females and males in the San socio-economic system. The penultimate episode, "Of Gods and Medicine Men", deals with ritual, dance, mythology and the role and function of the medicine man in a social context. The final episode, "The Beginning of the End", outlines the contemporary plight of the San following their assimilation and forced insertion into the Western money economy. The young men have gone to work on farms, are employed as trackers in the South African Defence Force, one is even shown driving a Mercedes Benz, the reward for being a Minister of the Turnhalle interim government in Namibia. The women are tempted with prostitution and often eke out an existence as lowly paid farm labour. This episode shows the permanent dwellings, the portable radios, inadequate water supplies and destitution brought upon them by 'civilisation'. Van der Post sketches the degeneration thus:

> But now they were in the grip of an inflexible environment where their water supplies were often tainted and where all their natural immunities completely deserted them. They were increasingly subject to disease and decay. Here in the areas which the chief represented, we found one of the last great indignities our civilisation had inflicted on primitive man - venereal disease, TB and drink.

Throughout the series, rock art is used as a reference point to sketch a historical background. Alternatively, it is used as tangible evidence on which to base complex interpretations of San mythology, ritual and their world view.

Unlike many of the earlier films on the San discussed above, there appears to be no apparent reconstruction of artifacts for the benefit of the camera. However, the same cannot be said for the action as portrayed on the screen. It is obvious that at least some of the action was staged for the benefit of the camera. During a hunting sequence (Episode 4: "Man the Hunter") two hunters are filmed from the front as they shoot their poisoned arrows at a Gemsbok. The camera then moves behind the hunters who are foregrounded in the frame over the wounded animal in the distance. This is but one fairly obvious instance of unacknowledged distortion, but it nevertheless raises questions about the authenticity of other sequences in the series.

There is a single authoritative narrator's presence throughout the series and at no stage are Bushmen given the opportunity of ad-

dressing the camera directly. The narration serves three functions. First, it complements the visual content with peripherally
relevant information. Second, it serves to interpret visual content
that would otherwise be confusing to the uninformed viewer.
Finally, it draws together complex and disparate visual elements
which could not hold their own without a narration linking them
together. The latter is particularly important in the episode on
the complex San mythology and the supernatural.

Van der Post's unquestionable sincerity and emotional involvement
in the series is mediated through both the tone of his voice and
the sometimes complex metaphorical use of language. However,
this emotion is almost self-reflexive as he leaves no doubt in the
viewers' mind that his presence in the film is more than simply a
part of an anthropological exercise - it is a personal crusade as
well. Unlike Marshall, however, the visual component of the film
does not demand the viewers' emotional involvement.

Although the sometimes complex metaphorical narration is
thought-provoking, it is nevertheless Van der Post's own personal
judgements as a literary figure and can be recognised as such.
Seldom can his 'authoritative' personal statements on myth and
the supernatural be objectively and scientifically verified. An
example of his narration will suffice in illustrating the point:

> To me, the most impressive thing about all this (the hunt) was
> that it was not merely the killing of an animal. It was not
> merely a question of food that was at stake because the
> hunter, as with so many of these stone age things, had
> acquired a two-dimensional role. In the role of the here and
> now he was the provider of food, but in the imagination, he
> was a provider of food for the spirit of the Bushmen. He
> represented in the Bushmen mind, that in the human being,
> which is in search of new meaning (Episode 6: "The Beginning
> of the End")

In summary, it has been possible to provide a critique of the film
by focussing separately on the visual content and the narration.
The visual content appears to do justice to what MacDougall has
termed the 'showing us something' brand of interpretive realism,
while the narration appears to adhere more to the 'telling a story'
brand of interpretive realism. The two components appear to

co-exist comfortably and, as with many of the earlier ethnographic films, it is possible to remove the narration from much of the film and replace it with a narration that adheres to the above theorised premises of ethnographic film-making.

In contrast, all three of the Marshall films provide a single and weighted interpretation of events governed by the quite blatant emotional attachment he has for the !Kung. Specific cases of misinterpretation as a direct result of this attachment are few and far between because, to highlight these, requires extensive independent, parallel research into the areas dealt with by the film. In one documented case, subsequent research into the extent to which the San were starving, proved **The Hunters** to be incorrect. The research showed that San subsistence techniques were sufficiently flexible to overcome temporary crises (Heider, 1972:32). This may have been an isolated misinterpretation by Marshall but it nevertheless raises doubts about the validity of a single authoritative documentary-type interpretation. With this in mind it is useful to provide a more empirical analysis of two of Marshall's most recent films, **Bushmen of the Kalahari** and **N!ai: The Story of a !Kung Woman.**

Both films exhibit a technical competence that is matched by few ethnographic films in this broad category. As a rule he adhered strictly to the wide angle, long duration shots which adds much to Marshall's accurate depiction of San hunting culture. The films show few, if any, jump cuts or overt distortion of reality through the post synchronization of sound. If they were employed they are not immediately apparent to the informed viewer.

Although inadvertent distortion of behaviour is always difficult to quantify, in **N!ai: The Story of a !Kung Woman,** N!ai herself manifests a marked degree of camera consciousness while being filmed as a young girl. At times she is coy and shy and her periodic glances towards the camera re-affirms that these are a result of, rather than independent of, the camera. However, Marshall does not hide this and herein lies the strength of his method of making explicit his specific interpretation of behaviour. In short, although we seldom see the presence of camera and crew, we are nevertheless implicitly aware of their presence through N!ai's reaction to them. This presence, however, does not remotely approach the concept of reflexivity as propounded by Ruby (1977).

There is little visual indication that sequences in either of the films were staged. In fact, it is the totally convincing and genuine portrayal of the 'real' that makes these films so powerful. In one scene in **N!ai: The Story of a !Kung Woman,** we see a fight between N!ai's daughter and her husband who suspects her of adultery. Not only are the subjects' violent action captured in the ensuing scuffle, but the spontaneity of the action required that the camera operator shoot the scene without prior preparation resulting in a marked degree of camera unsteadiness.

In **Bushmen of the Kalahari** there is a constant interplay between Marshall as anthropologist and the more specific social dynamics of the !Kung community. The film begins with shots of Harvard University where Marshall is seen interacting with members of his research team, while planning their intended expedition back to the !Kung reservation. The film appears to be as much a personal crusade or mission as it is a "tight integration of both ethnography and history" **(DER Catalogue, 1983).** The camera uses him as visual mediator which is maintained by his soothing narration. Marshall's role in both films therefore, is not clear-cut but can be interpreted on various levels. On the one hand his presence satisfies some of the methodological requirements of ethnographic presence, while on the other he plays a more central and complex role as authoritative interpreter of behaviour and events.

Both films make extensive use of footage from his short films previously mentioned. On occasion this proves problematic as there is a condensing of time. In **N!ai: The Story of a !Kung Woman,** Marshall partially overcomes this problem by using N!ai's growth from small girl to mature woman as a metonym for the logical historic development or demise of the entire !Kung community. In **The Hunters,** Marshall uses a film within a film to similar effect.

Perhaps the most convincingly redeeming feature of both films is the degree of holism employed. For example, we see a holistic treatment of a giraffe hunt including the socially integrative value of the subsequent sharing of the meat. In **N!ai: The Story of a !Kung Woman,** hunting and gathering is dealt with in a similar manner although the film content stresses the gradual demise of the !Kung social unit through their introduction to a Western money economy. N!ai is used throughout the film in the same way Marshall is used as a central reference point i.. **Bushmen of the Kalahari.** "... the film portrays the changes in !Kung society over three decades, it never loses sight of the individual N!ai. Through N!ai the story of the !Kung becomes more accessible, more personal, and ultimately more poignant" **(DER Catalogue,** 1983). In this regard, N!ai is seen as both a bone of contention in the community because she does not share her earnings with the rest of the community, as well as being the symbol of the degeneration of that community. Under the circumstances there is little need for Marshall to maintain a central role as interpreter of behaviour because of the logical progression of history in the !Kung community and the resultant juxtaposition between what they were and what they have become. Marshall's direct intervention as interpreter of events is limited to the posing of questions rather than overt statements of fact.

Marshall makes use of stylistic cinematic effects to place greater emotional emphasis on several sequences. In one such sequence in **N!ai: The Story of a !Kung Woman** there is a low angle shot of a horse munching the last few melons the !Kung community possesses. While Marshall is careful to stress the significance of keeping the horse alive so it can be used for hunting, the viewer is nevertheless made to feel sympathy for the animal instead of being made aware of the crisis that the lack of water poses for the community. On another occasion, Marshall chooses to highlight a heart-moving shot of a sheep licking the water dripping from a pipe. While this shot stresses the more general problem of thirst, it does little to explain the more specific problems of how the community eventually comes to terms with the situation.

Both **N!ai: The Story of a !Kung Woman** and **Bushmen of the Kalahari** provide adequate examples of both the strengths and problems inherent in interpretive realism. From this very general overview it is clear that the value of these films lies in the degree to which Marshall uses measured interpretive techniques and through careful editing, poses as many questions for the viewer as he provides answers.

Participant Realism

Participant realism is not one of Heider's categories, but has been enunciated by the authors to account for film-makers who often intuitively collapse many of the above categories into each other with a high degree of ethnographic presence, though **not** self-re-flexivity.   One such example is the San episode from **Vanishing Tribes of Africa,** an Anglia TV production made by Paul Myburgh and Anita van der Merwe.   Myburgh had previously lived amongst the San.   These film-makers "virtually formed a new band of left-overs (small San groups not part of the larger groups) related in one way or another ... like a large extended family of 24 people" **(The Star,** 13.2.84).   The film (i.e. the extracts screened on **Uit en Tuis** on 16.2.84) shows the adaption of the film-makers to the San way of life.   The ethnographic presence is established both by the two filmmakers who are seen in nearly every frame (one or other and sometimes both), but they are wearing the garb of the San as well.   This gives them a rather curious status: the film is not about the "Bushmen", but about them: how Paul learns to carve, throw a spear and dance.   The atmosphere is almost tranquil.   There is no sense of social dislocation, either of the two intruders or of the group with whom they reside.   The film is paced by sparse commentary on what they are doing, and what they feel.   Other sounds are singing, presumably by the San, though it appears to be overlaid rather than direct.

All in all, this is a brave attempt on the part of the film-makers to integrate themselves with their 'subjects' **(Vanishing Tribes of Africa),** learn indigenous crafts and reveal their process of socialization rather than to impose an alien perspective. However, it does not always come off, for the viewer is given too little information, either about the social relationships that deve-lop as a result of their intrusion or other activities in which everybody participates.

CONCLUSION

In terms of our equation:

(INTENT)-Anthropologist-Producer-Process-Subjects-Audience-(PUR-POSE)

We are able to conclude that ethnographic film-makers are increasingly becoming aware, either intuitively or explicitly, of the elements which make up a filmic ethnography.   The denegation of individuals and customs seen in early films on the

'Bushmen' which has been substituted by a romanticised portrayal followed by a selfcriticism on the part of the dominant social system, is indicative of changing INTENTIONS on the part of film-makers, a greater reliance on the guidance offered by anthropologists and other specialists, and a more sympathetic ethnographic understanding on the part of the Producer. Identification of Process remains a weak link and Subjects seem largely to remain the focus of, rather than participants in the production Process. This perpetuates the Us-drawing-the-line-around-Them power relationship. Films on the San thus remain films **about** rather than **of** the subject culture. Though more sympathetically portrayed, the with-holding of production knowledge from the San results in representatives of white Western culture assuming the Voice of Authority and interpreting on behalf of the indigenous culture. It is rare indeed that the subjects are allowed to address the camera directly.

The reasons for the continuing inequable power relationship relate to conceptions of the Audience and PURPOSE. Audiences, though often anthropologists, are outnumbered by less knowledgeable paying viewers (particularly when the programmes are transmitted on television). Thus it is necessary to use Laurens van der Post to present **Testament to the Bushmen** as he is a saleable figure who is coincidently knowledgeable about and has an empathy with the 'Bushmen'. The conventions of Western television often make no allowance for direct address by the subjects even if translated and dubbed. The camera is God and the narrator the Voice of Authority.

While the later films do have the propensity for enhancing intercultural and ethnographic understanding, they do so in terms of the attitudes and ideology of the dominant society. That the nature of cinematic depictions has changed over the years alters little: having destroyed the 'Bushmen' we can now afford to either romanticise them or blame their demise on the inexorable workings of Western culture and economy which know no boundaries. Such depiction should not, however, detract from the sincere INTENTIONS of producers but are indicative of a production-distribution-exhibition industry which now permits sympathetic portrayals.

Only the films of John Marshall and Van der Post try to remain true to the subjects though even these film-makers would seem to have been partly unaware of how form contributes to ideological content.

Like the films discussed in Chapter One, and the television series of **They Came From the East** examined in Chapter Two, it would appear that uncritical adherence to form, conventions and accepted codes does little to expose the underlying problems of ethnographic understanding. The dominant culture continues to reflect its cinematic subjects in terms of its own (if changing) ideology, and the dominated culture remains at the mercy of such distorted interpretations. They have no access whatsoever to the media other than through the ideologically conforming processes of production brought by the majority of film-makers concerned with making films 'about' the 'Bushmen'.

CONCLUSION

Given the pessimistic nature of much of the literature, it is not surprising that the films and television series examined in this study have been shown to be more propagandistic than ethnographic. The degree of ethnographicness has been shown to be markedly affected by the **context** of screening or transmission.

A comprehensive analysis would have to analyse the following production-exhibition chain if it is to account for the responses of both observer and observed:

(INTENT)-Anthropologist-Producer-Process-Subjects-Audience-(PURPOSE)

The above equation was applied to all the films studied, but specifically to **They Came From the East** and the various films on the San and the !Kung. With regard to the former, it was found that a greater knowledge of film theory and production principles, together with the ability of the Producer to negotiate the institutional and consensual discourse of the SABC, could have led to an acceptance of the programmes' interpretation from both 'white' and 'Indian' television audiences. The context in which the series was transmitted, however, led to divergent interpretations: political ('Indians') versus 'cultural' ('whites').

Television series about the Afrikaner are shown to be misleading. Operating from a liberal British perspective, with some exceptions, they tend to avoid a class analysis which would implicate both the British and English-speaking South Africans in the development of racial capitalism. Their analyses stereotype Afrikaners in terms of British myths which emphasise the 'humaneness' of 'the West' against the 'tough', 'relentless Afrikaner oppressor' of 'blacks'.

The response by the South African state to the 'lies' encoded in television series made by South African exiles and overseas companies has been a number of films made by the Department of Fo-

reign Affairs and Information. The former, mainly British television series, are misleading because of a blind adherence to the
discourse of 'objectivity' which skews interpretations in terms of
British liberalism. The latter, in contrast, are sophisticated propaganda which, in discrediting the supposed manipulative techniques of films critical of apartheid, proceed to apply similar techniques within a tautological textual double-talk aimed at persua-
ding the critical liberal discourse of the West of the 'positive' elements of South African development.

The result of the above is a struggle for meaning in the international media. The South African propaganda films are punting a
political message which is legitimised through the use of anthropological, ethnographic and very often development discourse.

The pseudo-scientific anthropological discourse which marks particular historical conjunctures is susceptible to radical reinterpreta-
tions as conditions change. A major example concerns the attitudes of film-makers who have documented the 'Bushmen' since
1912. From being a people with 'no God, no history and no morality', they are now depicted either within a romanticised and idea-
lised description which lauds the integration of these people with
their environment, or, they are examined in relation to the wider
social, political and economic pressures that are leading to the
disintegration of their culture and social groupings.

Unless a film is conscious of its epistemology - both cinematic
and anthropological - it can be easily co-opted by the wider political forces and turned into a weapon against or in defence of,
political strategies. As such, its ethnographic integrity is vitiated
and its scientific worth debased.

A filmic ethnography is not impossible, neither is a study **of** culture, although most explorations have been concerned with films
about cultures. A number of films and videos discussed in Chapter 2 (**On Becoming a Sangoma** and **I am Clifford Abrahams: This
is Grahamstown**) are pointers to the future for a more theoretical
approach, while **Testament to the Bushmen** and some of the more
recent Marshall films, are indications of the styles that can be
developed with regard to a more commercial distribution.

The question of **access** is important. We have outlined the dangers of observer-oriented productions. The observed, the subjects, are generally powerless and are at the mercy of the film-maker's integrity and ideological position. The subjects need to be given an opportunity to make films about themselves and to show these on television to a wider audience. The SABC has shown itself to be innovative in the area of ethnographic and anthropological film. Examples are **Portrait of a Marriage, Fighting Sticks** and **They Came From the East.** It is, however, unfortunate that the producers of some of these series often limit their analyses in terms of common sense media perceptions of an uninformed audience. Apart from this, they often have to tread a precarious political path for fear of falling foul of the SABC gatekeepers whose own practice would appear to be that of interpreting and enforcing the current political discourse of the SABC hierarchy.

The grid of conventional significations taken for granted by documentary film-makers further detracts from the validity of films dealing with people. It would be presumptious of us to insist that film-makers be forced into applying the criteria of an ethnographic filmography, but it is perhaps a comment on industry practice that **much research goes into subject matter, but almost none goes into methods of presentation and cinematic structure.** The well-worn lexicon of commercial documentary conventions is usually assumed to be appropriate for all tasks.

The discipline of ethnographic film needs to take problems of ideology into account. This study builds on previous work on the ideology-ethnographic couplet and developed specific scientific concepts to assist in a fuller understanding of film and video texts in relation to their **context,** both in terms of production and social practice. We have shown that film-makers who proceed without an awareness of the workings of ideology tend to encode more of their own values and prejudices in their films than they do of the people who they are filming. In such cases, an ethnographic film is really nothing more than the documentation of the meeting between two cultures. Such films do not reflect 'truth', 'reality', or a God's-eye-view of the subjects.

The most successful ethnographic film will result from a **sharing** of information and resources between the film-makers and their subjects. The inequable power relationship which normally governs production needs to be revised in the direction of the subjects who should be allowed to present themselves on screen using whatever cinematic or video techniques they think appropriate. The film-maker thus becomes a **facilitator** rather than an imposer.

POSTSCRIPT

This study has examined the role of ethnographic film as part of the Intergroup Relations Project of the Human Sciences Research Council. The results of that study were made public in July 1985. The report was a damning indictment on apartheid and came at a time when the state was facing an extended hegemonic crisis which had been growing since the establishment of the tricameral parliament in September 1983. A state of emergency was declared in thirty-six magisterial districts towards the end of the month. South Africa again found itself at war with itself.

The HSRC report was rejected by the government.

The State President said that he was sick and tired of Afrikaners and the National Party always being seen to be the cause of racial hatred. He claimed that apartheid was just a word that referred to a system which had existed way before the Afrikaans language had developed.

Two crucial points are lost on the State President. The first is that the majority of the 100 or so researchers who worked on the Project were Afrikaans-speaking, and that the report said nothing new. It merely sanctioned what liberal and radical scholars had been saying for decades.

The second point relates to the epistemological basis of the idea of 'intergroup relations'. This concept is itself part of the dominant myth-making process as it deflects what is essentially a political and economic struggle onto the domain of 'diplomacy'. The government and its para-statal bodies are constantly looking for ways to promote intergroup relations in terms of apartheid social relations. The HSRC found that despite this conceptual displacement, the fundamental stresses of our society could no longer be hidden under semantic categories legitimated by positivistic-oriented research or through stereotypes legitimised in practice through the media. Yet the government persists in talking about 'negotiation', 'minority rights' and 'democracy', as was done in the State President's address to the world at the Natal National Party Congress on 15 August 1985. The President underlined that the government would not tolerate the domination of one group by another (sic). By talking about intergroup relations, negotiation and consensus within its own highly culturally specific frame of reference, the government foreclosed the findings of the ASRC.

As such, it also has probably foreclosed the possibilities that might have been explored through the SABC as well. Exactly how much influence the HSRC study will have on government thinking will depend on how rifts within the cabinet are resolved. At the beginning of September 1985, the Foreign Minister, Mr Pik Botha, made the following startling announcement:

> I admit in years gone by we went too far with legislative measures and concentrated too much on fragmentation and compartmentalisation of our communities. We have changed our attitude in this respect. We now see clearly that we have a lot in common and instead of concentrating solely on the differences we are concentrating on what we have in common.

Just how pervasive this attitude is in the cabinet is not clear. What is clear is that the SABC, administered as it is under the Department of Foreign Affairs and Information, is partly being used to propagate the reformist position embodied in Pik Botha's statement. The strength of the reformists and the success of their strategies will only be measured by history.

BIBLIOGRAPHY

ALTHUSSER, L. 1971. **Lenin and Philosophy.** New York:Monthly Review Press.

ALTHUSSER, L. and BALIBAR, E. 1971. **Reading Capital.** London: New Left Books.

ASCH, T. 1975. Using Film in Teaching Anthropology: One Pedagogical Approach, in P. HOCKINGS (ed.): **Principles of Visual Anthropology.** The Hague: Mouton.

BALACHOFF, D. Psycho Psychology of Film and Video. Paper presented at **FILM '81, British Kinomatograph, Sound and Television Society Conference,** London.

BARTHES, R. 1973. **Mythologies.** London: Paladin.

BAZIN, A. 1967. **What is Cinema? Part 1.** Berkeley, University of California Press.

BOZZOLI, B. 1981. **The Political Nature of a Ruling Class: Capital and Ideology in South Africa 1890-1933.** London: Routledge and Kegan Paul.

DER, 1982. **FILMS FROM DER.** Watertown: Documentary Education Resources.

DICKSON, W. 1984. Die Vroue Revolusie. In K.G. Tomaselli: **Documentary, Ethnographic Film and the Problem of Realism.** Grahamstown: Department of Journalism and Media Studies, Rhodes University.

CAHIERS DU CINEMA. 1970. John Ford's Young Mr Lincoln, p.6.

CINEASTE, 1976. Clandestine Filming in South Africa - An Interview with Nana Mahomo. 7(3), 18-23.

CRANKSHAW, P., WILLIAMS, A. and HAYMAN, G. 1983. To Educate, Entertain and Inform. The Meyer Commission into TV. **The SAFTTA Journal,** 3(1&2), 20-27.

ECO, U. Quoted in M.C. HECK, 1980: The Ideological Dimension of Media Messages. In **Culture, Media, Language.** London: Hutchinson in association with the Centre for Contemporary Cultural Studies.

ECO, U. 1976. **A Theory of Semiotics.** London: MacMillan.

ELLUL, J. 1964. **The Technological Society.** New York: Vintage Books.

FABIAN, J. 1971. Language, History, and Anthropology. **Journal of the Philosophy of the Social Sciences.** 1, 19-47.

FELDMAN, S. 1977. Viewer, Viewing, Viewed: A Critique of Subject-Generated Documentary. **Journal of the University Film Association,** 29(4), 23-38.

FILM LIBRARY QUARTERLY. 1976. Nana Mahomo Interviewed. 9(1), 11-14.

FISKE, J. 1982. **Introduction to Communication Studies.** London: Methuen.

FOURIE, P. 1981. How can the South African Film Industry be Rescued From its Plight? **Rapport,** 21 June.

GAVSHON, H. 1980. **Ideology and Film: An Examination of Films made for Black Audiences in South Africa.** Final Year Dissertation, School of Dramatic Art, University of the Witwatersrand.

GOLDSCHMIDT, W. 1972. **Ethnographic Film: Definition and Exogesis.** Washington: PIEF.

GRIERSON, J. Quoted in C. WILLIAMS (ed.), 1980: **Realism and the Cinema.** London: Routledge and Kegan Paul in association with the British Film Institute.

GRIERSON, J. in ROTHA, P. 1936. **Documentary Film.** London: Faber and Faber, 1-14.

HALL, S.J. 1976. Last Grave at Dimbaza. **Film Library Quarterly,** 9(1), 15-18.

HALL, S., CRITCHER, C., JEFFERSON, T., CLARKE, J. and ROBERTS, B. 1978. **Policing the Crisis: Mugging the State and Law and Order.** London: MacMillan.

HARRISON, D. 1981. **The White Tribe of Africa: South Africa in Perspective.** Johannesburg: MacMillan.

HAYMAN, G. and TOMASELLI, R.E. 1986. Technology in the Service of Ideology: the First 50 Years of Broadcasting in South Africa. In K.G. TOMASELLI, TOMASELLI, R.E. and MULLER, J. (eds): **Addressing the Nation: Studies in the South African Media,** Vol. 1. Durban: Anchor Publications.

HEIDER, K.G. 1972. **Ethnographic Film.** Austin: University of Texas Press.

HEIDER, K.G. 1983. Fieldwork with a Camera. **Studies in Visual Communication,** 9(1), 2-10.

HECK, M.C. 1980. The ideological dimensions of media messages. In **Culture, Media, Language.** London: Hutchinson in association with the Centre for Contemporary Cultural Studies.

HOCKINGS, P. (ed.) 1975. **Principles of Visual Anthropology.** The Hague: Mouton.

HUTTENBACK, R.A. 1976. **Racism and Empire.** Ithaca: University Press.

JORDAN, W. 1974. The Myth of the Savage. In R.A. MAYNARD (ed.) **Africa on Film.** New Jersey: Hayden Books.

KAPLAN, E. 1983. **Women and Film - Both Sides of the Camera.** New York: Methuen.

KUHN, T.S. 1977. **The Essential Tension: Selected Studies in Scientific Tradition and Change.** Chicago: University of Chicago Press. See Kuhn's essay on Logic of Discovery.

KUPER, H. 1960. **Indian People in Natal.** University of Natal Press, Natal.

LEACOCK, R. 1971. Condensed Dogma of one Film-maker. In G.R. LEVIN (ed.): **Documentary Explorations.** New York: Doubleday.

LE GRANGE, L. 1980. Persverantwoordelikheid Gesien van die Kant van die Owerheid. **Ecquid Novi,** 1(2), 1980, 139-149.

LEWIS-WILLIAMS, J.D. 1983. An Ethnographic Interpretation of a Rock Painting from Barkley East. **Humanitas,** 9(3), 245-250.

MACDOUGALL, D. 1969. Prospects of the Ethnographic Film. **Film Quarterly,** 23(2), 16-30.

MACDOUGALL, D. 1975. Beyond Observational Cinema. In HOCKINGS, **op. cit.,** 109-124.

MACDOUGALL, D. 1978. Ethnographic Film: Failure and Promise. **Annual Review of Anthropology,** No. 7 Palo Alto: Annual Reviews, 405-425.

MACIVER, R.M. 1931. **Society: Its Structure and Changes.** New York: Long and Smith.

McALLISTER, P. and HAYMAN, G. 1984. **Shixini December.** Paper presented at 2nd Carnegie Inquiry into Poverty and Development in Southern Africa, University of Cape Town.

MAIN COMMITTEE, HSRC INVESTIGATION INTO INTERGROUP RELATIONS, 1985. **The South African Society: Realities and Future Prospects.** Pretoria: HSRC.

MALINOWSKI, B. 1922. **Argonauts of the Western Pacific.** New York: EP Dutton.

MARKS, S. 1981. 'Bold, thievish, and not to be trusted': Racial Stereotypes in South Africa in Historical Perspective. **History Today,** 31, 15-21.

MARSHALL, L. and BIESELE, M. (Undated) N/UM Tchai: **The Ceremonial Dance of the !Kung Bushmen. A Study Guide.** Mass: Documentary Educational Resources.

MAUGHAN BROWN, D. 1983. The Noble Savage in Anglo-Saxon Colonial Ideology, 1950-1980: 'Masai' and 'Bushmen' in popular fiction. **English in Africa,** 10(2), 55-78.

MAYNARD, R.A. 1974. **Africa on Film: Myth and Reality.** New Jersey: Hayden Books.

MERCER, J. 1979. **Glossary of Film Terms.** Houston: University Film Association.

MERRELYN, M. and EMERY, F. 1980. The Vacuous Vision: The TV Medium. **Journal of the University Film Association,** 32(1&2), 27-32.

MILIBAND, R. 1973. **The State in Capitalist Society.** London: Quartet.

MONACO, J. 1981. **How to read a Film.** New York: Oxford University Press.

MORIN, E. 1962. Preface in DE HEUSCH, L. **The Cinema and Social Science; a Survey of Ethnographic and Sociological Films.** Report and Papers in the Social Sciences 16. Paris: UNESCO.

MULLER, J. 1983. Culture and Education in Southern Africa. Paper presented to the **Cultural Studies Workshop.** Gaborone: Foundation for Education with Production.

NICHOLS, B. 1981. **Ideology and the Image.** Bloomington: Indiana University Press.

PHILLIPS, B.S. 1969. **Sociology: Social Structure and Social Changes.** London: MacMillan.

POPPER, K. 1963. **Conjectures and Refutations: The Growth of Scientific Knowledge.** London: Routledge and Kegan Paul.

REICHLIN, S. 1974. **Tug of War.** Mass: Documentary Educational Resources.

REICHLIN, S. 1974. **The Lion Game.** Mass: Documentary Educational Resources.

REICHLIN, S. 1975. **A Rite of Passage. Film Notes.** Mass: Documentary Educational Resources.

REICHLIN, S. 1974. **Bitter Lemons. A Study Guide.** Mass: Documentary Educational Resources.

REICHELIN, S. 1974. **The Meat Fight. A Study Guide.** Mass: Documentary Educational Resources.

ROTHA, P. 1936. **Documentary Film.** London: Faber and Faber.

ROUCH quoted in HEIDER, 1983, **op. cit.**

RUBY, J. 1971. Toward an Anthropological Cinema. **Film Comment, 7,** 35-40.

RUBY, J. 1975. Is an Ethnographic Film a Filmic Ethnography? **Studies in the Anthropology of Visual Communication,** 2(2), 104-111.

RUBY, J. 1976. Anthropology and Film: the Social Science Implications of Regarding Film as Communication. **Quarterly Review of Film Studies, 1,** 436-445.

RUBY, J. 1977. The Image Mirrored: Reflexivity and the Documentary Film. **Journal of the University Film Association.** 29(1), 3-18.

SAFFORD, K. 1981. Peter Davis' Film View of South Africa: An American Review. **Critical Arts,** 2(1), 94-97.

SAUL, J.S. and GELB, S. 1981. **The Crisis in South Africa: Class Defence, Class Revolution.** New York: Monthly Review Press.

SILBERBAUER, G.B. 1981. **Hunter and Habitat in the Central Kalahari Desert.** Cambridge: Cambridge University Press.

SILBERBAUER, G.B. 1965. **Report to the Government of Bechuanaland on the Bushmen Survey.** Bechuanaland Press, Mafeking.

SMELSER, N.J. 1967. **Sociology: An introduction.** New York: Wiley.

STEENVELD, L. 1984. **A Place Called Soweto.** In Tomaselli (1984c), 46-49.

STEYN, M.T. 1981. **Report of the Steyn Commission of Inquiry into the Mass Media.** Republic of South Africa, RP/89/1981.

THERBORN, G. 1980. **The Ideology of Power and the Power of Ideology.** London: Verso.

TOBIAS, P.V. 1978. **The Bushmen.** Cape Town: Human and Rousseau.

TOMASELLI, K.G. 1980a. Ethnographic Film and the Problem of Ideology. Paper presented at the **Conference of the Association for Sociology in Southern Africa,** Lesotho.

TOMASELLI, K.G. 1980b. Ideology and Censorship in South African Cinema. **Critical Arts,** 1(2), 1-14.

TOMASELLI, K.G. 1981a. **The South African Film Industry.** Johannesburg: African Studies Institute, University of the Witwatersrand.

TOMASELLI, K.G. 1981b. Six Days in Soweto: Can Propaganda be Truth? **Ecquid Novi,** 2(1), 49-56.

TOMASELLI, K.G. 1983a. Strategies for an Independent Radical Cinema in South Africa. **Marang,** 3, 51-88.

TOMASELLI, K.G. 1983b. **Ideology and Cultural Production in South African Cinema.** Ph.D Thesis, University of the Witwatersrand.

TOMASELLI, K.G. 1984a. Visual Images of South African Communities. Paper presented to the **38th Conference of the University Film and Video Association,** Virginia.

TOMASELLI, K.G. 1984b. The South African Film Industry: Cultural Protection and Ideological Trade-Offs 1940-1981. **Cinema Canada.**

TOMASELLI, K.G. 1984c. **Documentary, Ethnographic Film and the Problem of Realism.** Grahamstown: Dept. of Journalism, Rhodes University.

TOMASELLI, K.G. 1985. Progressive film and video in South Africa. **Media Development,** 32(3), 15-17.

TOMASELLI, K.G., TOMASELLI, R.E. and MULLER, J. 1986. **Addressing the Nation: Studies in the South African Media,** Vol. 1. Durban: Anchor Publications.

TOMASELLI, R.E. 1983. **The Indian Flower Sellers of Johannesburg.** MA Thesis, University of the Witwatersrand.

VAN ZYL, J.A.F. 1980a. 'No God, No Morality, No History': South African Ethnographic Film. **Critical Arts,** 1(1), 32-37.

VAN ZYL, J.A.F. 1980b. **They Came From the East.** Valuable Ethnography, **The SAFTTA Journal,** 1(1), 22-23.

VAN ZYL, J.A.F. 1981. Ethnographic Film Festival. **Critical Arts,** 1(4), 46-48.

VENIS, R. 1980. Seeing is Believing. **The BKSTS Journal,** 62(3), 98-100.

VERON, E. quoted in HECK, **op. cit.**

VOSS, A.E. 1982. Thomas Pringle and the Image of the Bushmen. **English in Africa,** 9(1), 15-28.

WILKINS, I. and STRYDOM, H. 1978. **The Super-Afrikaners: Inside the Afrikaner Broederbond.** Johannesburg: Jonathan Ball.

WILLIAMS, R. 1974. **Television: Technology and Cultural Form.** Glasgow: Fontana/Collins.

WILLIAMS, C. (ed.) 1980. **Realism and the Cinema.** London: Routledge and Kegan Paul.

WORTH, S. 1981. **Studying Visual Communication.** Philadelphia: University of Pennsylvania Press.

WORTH, S. and ADAIR, J. 1972. **Through Navajo Eyes: An Exploration in Film Communication and Anthropology.** Bloomington: Indiana University Press.

WRIGHT quoted in MAUGHAN BROWN, **op. cit.**

YOUNG, C. 1975. Observational Cinema. In P. HOCKINGS (ed.) **Principles of Visual Anthropology.** The Hague: Mouton.

FILMOGRAPHY
List of films viewed in the course of this study

Where possible, a list of critiques have been provided for readers wishing to follow up specific films. The information contained below is not complete, for it was often difficult to determine date of release, etc.

The Abakwetha, Ray Phoenix, 35mm, estimated 1956.

African Jim, Warrior Films, Johannesburg. Donald Swanson, 1949. 16mm, Black and White.

Africa Mosaic, Department of Foreign Affairs and Information, 16mm, 1980.

Against the Swirl of Time, Phoenix Productions, Ray Phoenix. 16mm, Colour.

Die Afrikaanse Taal, NFB, Willem Viljoen, 1972.

An Argument About a Marriage, John Marshall, DER, 1968. Study Guide available from DER.

And Then Came The English, Independent Film Centre (IFC) and SABC-TV, Lionel Friedberg, 7 episodes, 1983.

Amazulu Wedding Ceremonies, African Film Productions, 16mm.

Awake From Mourning, Chris Austin, Maggie Magaba Trust, 16mm, 1981. See Tomaselli (1983a).

Axe Fight, Napoleon Chagnon and Timothy Asch, DER, 1971.

Baobab Play, John Marshall, DER, 1974. Study Guide available from DER.

Bopelo, Brunnon Des Lebens, Protea Films, Werner Grunbauer, 35mm.

Bitter Lemons, John Marshall, DER, 1971. See Reichlin (1974).

The Bushmen. See The Denver Africa Expedition.

The Bushmen of the Kalahari, Robert Young, National Geographic Society, 1974.

Die Boesman Boogmaker, R Johnston, 1964.

Children Throw Toy Assegais, John Marshall, DER, 1974. Study Guide available from DER.

The Chopi Timbila Dance, Pennsylvania State University, Andrew Tracey and Gei Zantzinger. See Van Zyl (1981).

The Colour Bar, BBC-TV, David Wheeler, 16mm.

Colourful Courtship, Kurt Baum, 1958.

Cultural Identity, IFC, Dept of Information, Lionel Friedberg.

A Curing Ceremony, John Marshall, Documentary Educational Resources (DER), 1969.

Dances of Southern Africa, Pennsylvania State University, Gei Zantzinger, 1968.

Debe's Tantrum, John Marshall, DER, 1972.

The Defiant White Tribe.

Denver African Expedition, Universities of Denver and Cape Town and the South African Museum, Ernest Cradle and Grant John, estimated 1912. See Van Zyl (1980a).

Dingaka, Jamie Uys, 1964, 35mm.

Discover Sannyas, School of Dramatic Art, Wits University/Clare Schwartzburg, video, 1983.

The Dispossessed, Gavin Younge, 16mm, 1980.

The End of Dialogue, Overseas Productions.

Fighting Sticks, SABC TV, Tommy McLelland, 2 episodes, 1983.

From the Assegai to the Javelin, Killarney, estimated 1970.

Gandhi, Richard Attenborough, 1983.

Gansbaai, 'n Vissers se Gemeenskap, NFB, Henry Nel.

A Group of Women, John Marshall, DER, undated.

Die Hart van 'n Stad, NFB, Hans Wagner, 1964.

The Heart of Apartheid, BBC-TV, Hugh Burnett.

Hindu Fire Walking in South Africa, Ray Phoenix.

The Hunters, John Marshall, 1958. See Heider (1972).

I Am Clifford Abrahams: This is Grahamstown, Department of Journalism and Media Studies, Rhodes University, Grahamstown, 1984. Keyan Tomaselli, Cliffie Abrahams, Graham Hayman and Don Pinnock.

Ikaya, SA Institute of Architects, Glen Gallagher, 1976. See Tomaselli (1980a).

Indians in South Africa, NFB, John Fennel.

Indigenous Healers of Africa, Len Holdstock, University of Witwatersrand, 1980.

A Joking Relationship, John Marshall, DER, 1969.

Die Kaapse Maleiers, NFB, Mihaly Brunda.

Kalahari Klaskamer, R Johnston, 1964.

!Kung Bushmen Hunting Equipment, John Marshall, DER, 1966.

Kuns van die Rotswande, Killarney, Rod Stewart, 1970.

The Land of the Red Blanket.

Last Grave at Dimbaza, Nana Mahamo, 1970s. See **Cineaste** (1976).

Lion Game, John Marshall, DER, 1969. See Reichlin (1974).

The Long Search, BBC-TV, Ronald Eyre.

My Buurt, My Trots, NFB for the SA Administration of Coloured Affairs, 1974.

Mapadimeng, Department of Foreign Affairs and Information, 1973.

The Meat Fight, John Marshall, DER, 1974. See Reichlin (1974).

The Melon Tossing Game, John Marshall, DER, undated.

Mbira, Pennsylvania State University, Andrew Tracey and Gei Zantzinger, 6 titles, 1975.

Men Bathing, John Marshall, DER, 1972.

Murudruni, Commercial Radio Corporation Studios, Johannesburg, Derek Lamport. Estimated 1960s. 16mm, Colour.

Nai: The Story of a !Kung Woman, Documentary Educational Resources, John Marshall, 1982.

On Becoming a Sangoma, Dept of Psychology, University of Witwatersrand, Len Holdstock and Keyan Tomaselli, 1980.

A Place Called Soweto, Department of Foreign Affairs and Information, 1979. See Steenveld, (1984).

Playing with Scorpions, John Marshall, DER, 1972.

Pondo Story, South African Information Department and Chamber of Mines, Ray Gettermo. 16mm, Monochrome.

Portrait of a Marriage, SABC-TV, Gavin Levinson.

Radio Bantu, NFB, estimated 1970. See Heider (1972).

Remnants of a Race, Killarney Films, Black and White, negative, estimated 1940.

Reverand Jaques ethnographic footage. Lodged in the National Film Archives. 16mm, Black and White.

A Rite of Passage, John Marshall, DER, 1952. See Reichlin (1975).

Rock Art Treasures, Killarney Films, Department of Foreign Affairs and Information, 16mm, 35mm, Rod Stewart, 1970.

Siliva the Zulu, University of Florence, Attilio Gatti and Lidio Cipriani, estimated 1926. See Van Zyl (1980a), though this reference is fairly inaccurate.

Shixini December, Rhodes University, Graham Hayman and Pat McAllister, 1984. See McAllister, P and Hayman, G (1984).

Six Days in Soweto, ITV, Anthony Thomas, 1977. See Tomaselli (1981b).

Solution to the Dilemma of a Plural Society, Department of Information, 1977.

South Africa Loves Jesus, BBC-TV, Hugh Burnett.

The South African Experience, ITV, Anthony Thomas, 1977.

South African Native Life.

South Africa's Performing Arts, Raymond Hancock Films, Department of Foreign Affairs and Information, Roger Harris, 1970.

Soweto, Johannesburg City Council, Sven Persson, 1972. See Tomaselli (1980a).

Swerwers van die Sandveld, Killarney Films, Department of Education, Art and Science, estimated 1940. See Van Zyl (1980a).

Sun People, SATOUR, T V Bulpin, 1956.

Testament to the Bushmen, Paul Bellinger, 1983.

There Lies Your Land, Raymond Hancock Films. Raymond Hancock, 1975.

They Came From the East, IFC and SABC-TV, Lionel Friedberg, 6 episodes, 1980. See Van Zyl, (1980b).

This We Can Do For Justice and Peace, Kevin Harris, SACC, 1981. See Tomaselli (1983a).

To Act a Lie, Department of Information, 1978.

The Tribal Identity, IFC and SABC-TV, Lionel Friedberg, 8 episodes, 1977.

Tug-of-War, Timothy Asch and Napoleon Chagnon, DER, 1971. See Reichlin (1974).

Venda: 'n Nuwe Staat, Department of Information, 1980.

Die Vroue Revolusie, Department of Information, David Shreeve, 1977. See Dickson (1984).

The Wasp Nest, John Marshall, DER, 1973.

The White Laager, UNESCO, Peter Davis, 1977. See Safford (1981).

White Roots in Africa, Department of Foreign Affairs and Information, Jans Rautenbach, 1978.

The White Tribe of Africa, BBC-TV, David Dimbleby, 1981. See Harrison (1981).

UIPTN News Report on Gangsterism in the Cape Flats, Cliff Bestall.

Who is Vasco Mutwa, Department of Foreign Affairs and Information, 1970.

A World of Difference, Independent Film Centre, Chamber of Mines. 16mm.

INDEX

- 123 -

scientific   16
undercoding   18, 36, 79
verbal (includes narration and Voice of Authority)   13, 30, 33,
41, 44, 46, 61-63, 65, 67-69, 71-72, 73, 85, 92, 94-95, 100
communication   5, 7
inter-cultural   5, 40, 51-52, 100
means of   4, 16, 44-45
mode of   16
culture   1, 11, 14, 15, 27, 28, 32, 33, 40, 41, 45, 74, 81-85
definition   19
Cultural Identity (Film)   40, 117
Curing Ceremony, A (Film)   90, 117

Debe's Tantrum (Film)   90, 117
Defiant White Tribe, The (Film)   57, 58, 65, 117
Denver Africa Expedition (Film)   77, 79, 81-85, 117
documentary   1, 8, 10, 13, 18, 19, 21-23, 31, 32, 34, 35, 38, 39
41, 44, 45, 64, 75
definitions   18-19, 21, 57

End of Dialogue (Film)   65, 117
ethnography   8, 10-12
definitions   8, 10-16, 78
ethnographic film   7, 8, 11, 12, 15, 18, 26, 30, 34, 39, 78
definitions   9-13, 17, 34, 37, 39, 54
fragmentary   89-91
historical   84, 97
institutional   33, 48-49, 53
instructional   80, 85-89
naïve   78, 80, 81-85, 89, 90
power relation between film crew and subjects   16-18, 30, 33,
35, 46, 100, 104, 105
ethnographicness, degrees of   38, 39, 55, 102
ethnographic presence   28-29, 37, 39, 43-45, 52, 90, 96, 99
ethnographic present   30, 37, 39
ethnographic production principles   26-30
ethnographic film semiotics   9, 12, 15, 37
experience   34

MacDougall, David   11, 12, 14, 29, 34, 78, 79, 91, 95
Marshall, John   31, 90, 96-98, 101, 103
Meat Fight, The (Film)   90, 119
Melon Tossing Game, The (Film)   90, 119
Men Bathing (Film)   90, 119
mysticism   30, 33
myth   7, 36, 48, 51, 59-61, 63, 71, 79, 95, 105
   definition   3-5
mythology   94, 95

N!ai: The Story of a !Kung Woman (Film)   77, 90, 91, 96-98, 119
Ndando Yawusiwana (Film)   24

observational cinema   34, 78-79, 91
On Becoming a Sangoma (Film)   18, 25, 27-29, 36, 103, 119

Place Called Soweto, A (Film)   4, 20, 21, 64, 66, 72, 119
Playing with Scorpions (Film)   90, 119
Portrait of a Marriage (TV)   104, 119
propaganda   3, 4, 8, 23, 31, 32, 33, 35, 36, 37, 40, 45, 72, 76,
   77, 80, 102-103
   definition   35

racism   61, 74, 80, 81, 88-89, 93, 105
Radio Bantu (Film)   33, 119
reality   6, 7, 18-24, 26-27, 31, 64-73, 79
realism   18, 19-24
   descriptive   77-79
   interpretive   79, 80, 89, 91-98
   native   80
   neo-   21
   participant   98-99
realistic   22, 87
reflexivity (including methodology and process)   11, 13-17, 29,
   34, 37, 42, 44-45, 51, 95, 96
Remnants of a Race (Film)   80-85, 119
Rite of Passage (Film)   90, 120
Rock Art Treasures (Film)   30, 32, 80, 85-89, 120
Rotha, Paul   18-19, 22, 33-34, 64
Ruby, Jay   2, 10-15, 17, 29, 52, 96

South African Broadcasting Corporation (SABC)   23, 40, 43,
   45, 46, 49, 51, 53, 54, 55, 86, 102, 104, 106
SA Indian Council (SAIC)   42-43
science/scientific   6, 7, 10, 13, 16, 26, 28, 29, 34, 37, 44, 77,
   103, 104
Solution to the Dilemma of a Plural Society (Film)   64, 71, 120
South African Experience (including Six Days in Soweto) (TV)
   32, 34, 62, 120
South Africa Loves Jesus (Film)   57, 120
South African Mosaic (Film)   20
South Africa's Performing Arts (Film)   32, 74, 120

technique   13, 24, 29, 30, 33, 34, 44, 51, 65-68
technology   16, 23, 26, 27, 28, 29, 31, 34, 37, 51
Testament to the Bushmen (TV)   77, 91-96, 100, 103
They Came From the East (TV)   23, 33, 36, 39-56, 101, 102,
   104, 121
This We Can Do For Justice and Peace (Film)   20, 121
There Lies your Land (Film)   31, 120
Tribal Identity, The (TV)   11, 18, 23, 32, 33, 36, 40, 121
truth   1, 14, 18-23, 26, 30, 51-52, 54, 64-73, 75, 78, 104
To Act a Lie (Film)   21, 64-72, 74, 121
Tug of War (Film)   90, 121

Van Zyl, John   2, 8, 31, 33, 47, 80
Van der Post, Laurence   31, 91-95, 100, 101
Vanishing Tribes of Africa (TV)   99
Venda: 'n Nuwe Staat (Film)   31, 72, 121
Vrouerevolusie, Die (Film)   31, 121

Wasp Nest, The (Film)   90, 121
White Laager (Film)   57, 58, 121
White Roots in Africa (Film)   20, 21, 64, 67, 74, 121
White Tribe of Africa (TV)   4, 32, 57-64, 73-76
Who is Vasco Mutwa? (Film)   30, 121
Worth, Sol   5, 9, 11, 15-17, 63, 80